Internationalism and Nationalism in European Political Thought

Internationalism and Nationalism in European Political Thought

Carsten Holbraad

INTERNATIONALISM AND NATIONALISM IN EUROPEAN POLITICAL THOUGHT
© Carsten Holbraad, 2003

First published 2003 by
PALGRAVE MACMILLAN™
175 Fifth Avenue, New York, N.Y. 10010 and
Houndmills, Basingstoke, Hampshire, England RG21 6XS
Companies and representatives throughout the world.

PALGRAVE MACMILLAN is the global academic imprint of the Palgrave Macmillan division of St. Martin's Press, LLC and of Palgrave Macmillan Ltd. Macmillan® is a registered trademark in the United States, United Kingdom and other countries. Palgrave is a registered trademark in the European Union and other countries.

ISBN 1–40396–123–9 hardback

Library of Congress Cataloging-in-Publication Data
Holbraad, Carsten
Internationalism and nationalism in European political thought/
Carsten Holbraad.
        p. cm.
    Includes bibliographical references.
    ISBN 1–40396–123–9
        1. Internationalism. 2. Nationalism. 3. International cooperations.
4. Political science—Europe. I. Title.

JC362.H488 2003
320.54′094—dc21   2002030835

A catalogue record for this book is available from the British Library.

Design by Newgen Imaging Systems (P) Ltd., Chennai, India.

First edition: March, 2003
10 9 8 7 6 5 4 3 2 1

Printed in the United States of America.

To Anna, Samuel and Alexander

Contents

List of Tables

List of Abbreviations

BENELUX	Union of Belgium, Netherlands and Luxembourg
CDU	Christian Democratic Union
CIA	Central Intelligence Agency
COMECON/CMEA	Council for Mutual Economic Assistance
COMINFORM	Communist Information Agency
COMINTERN	Communist International
CPSU	Communist Party of the Soviet Union
DDR	German Democratic Republic (East Germany)
EC	European Community
ECSC	European Coal and Steel Community
EDC	European Defense Community
EEC	European Economic Community
EFTA	European Free Trade Area
EPC	European Political Cooperation
EPU	European Payments Union
ERE	National Radical Union
EU	European Union
FF	Fundamental Freedoms
FYROM	Former Yugoslav Republic of Macedonia
GATT	General Agreement on Tariffs and Trade
HR	Human Rights
IBRD	International Bank for Reconstruction and Development
IMF	International Monetary Fund
NATO	North Atlantic Treaty Organization
NPD	National Democratic Party
NSF	National Socialist Front
OECD	Organization for Economic Cooperation and Development
OEEC	Organization for European Economic Cooperation

PASOK	Panhellenic Socialist Movement
SCANDILUX	Forum for Social Democrats from the Scandinavian and BENELUX countries
SDP	Social Democratic Party (Danish)
SPD	Social Democratic Party (German)
UK	United Kingdom
US	United States
USSR	Union of Soviet Socialist Republics
UN	United Nations
UNESCO	United Nations Economic and Social Council
WEU	Western European Union
WTO	Warsaw Treaty Organization
WWI	First World War
WWII	Second World War

Preface

This book was conceived in the late 1980s, when Europe was still divided by the cold war. In both Eastern and Western Europe, international relations could then be seen in terms of an interaction between internationalism and nationalism. In the East, the interaction was essentially between the Soviet version of socialist internationalism and the various nationalist reactions of other members of the projected Socialist Commonwealth. In the West, it was largely between liberal and social democratic forms of internationalism, expressed primarily in the integrationist pursuits of the European Community, and nationalist inclinations, reflected in much of the opposition to such endeavors.

The petering out of the cold war and the collapse of the Soviet Union put an end to the division of Europe and the bifurcation of ideological debate. While the communist form of socialist internationalism hastily retreated, an invigorated liberal internationalism swept across most of Europe. At the same time, various types of nationalism, for long curbed by the polarizing forces of the cold war, came to the forefront again, in particular among the former communist countries and within the multinational states, especially the former Soviet Union and Yugoslavia. The conflict between the prevailing internationalism and resurgent nationalism came to a point in the war over Kosovo, in which NATO forces, acting in the name of liberal internationalist principles of human rights for ethnic minorities, fought a nationalist Serbia engaged in the suppression of a local ethnic group.

As in the past, the international order of Europe in the future is likely to be conditioned by the interaction between competing trends of internationalism and diverse kinds of nationalism. The aim of this book is to distinguish various forms and types of each; to indicate their origins, trace their development and analyze their interplay; and to present their manifestations and note their influence in European politics, in particular during the second half of the twentieth century.

The book was written while I was at the London School of Economics and Political Science, as a Visiting Fellow first at the Center for International Studies and then at the European Institute, and later as an Academic Visitor in the Department of International Relations. I am grateful to the School for the hospitality it offered me when I returned to London after many years in other parts of the world. Of the numerous relevant activities in which I have participated at the LSE, the most stimulating has been a seminar series on International Society after the Cold War, which James Mayall conducted in the Department of International Relations in 1993–5 as part of a Ford Foundation project about post–cold war international relations.

Of the many members of the Department of International Relations who have taken an interest in my work, I would like to mention especially Margot Light and Christopher Coker, who read particular draft chapters and made critical comments. The book has also benefited greatly from constructive criticism and helpful suggestions by Jack Spence and Brian Porter as well as by Peter Wilson, editor of the Palgrave Series on the History of International Thought, and David Long, member of the advisory board of the series, all of whom read the final draft.

Finally, I gratefully acknowledge my debt to the Nuffield Foundation, which under its small-grants scheme financed several useful visits to various European countries at the early stages of my research.

An earlier version of the first chapter of the book appeared under the title "Peace and War in Conservative Internationalist Thought" in C. Bell (ed.), *Nation, Region and Context: Studies in Peace and War in Honour of Professor T. B. Millar*, Strategic and Defence Studies Center, Research School of Pacific and Asian Studies, The Australian National University, Canberra, 1995.

London   C. H.
November 2001

Introduction

Internationalism may be described as the ideology of international bonding. However, the bonds that link states, nations and groups of individuals and make up the multidimensional international society of the modern world are of several kinds and join together a broad variety of parties. They are intergovernmental as well as transnational and sometimes, especially at regional and local levels, also supranational bonds, and may link sovereigns, governments, nongovernmental organizations, commercial firms, political parties, popular movements and other groups of people. Moreover, the general purposes of such bonding differ greatly. The aim may be to maintain or develop the existing order of international society, or to change that order and transform international society in some way or other.

Thus, there are several kinds of internationalism, each of which may comprise two or more types. A basic distinction is between the conservative and the more progressive. Though all of them pertain to international society by virtue of their extraction from various sets of international bonds, progressive internationalism often tends to transcend the confines of that society. Whether it is liberal or socialist, it may go beyond the state-centric structure of international society and, in its ultimate goals and more ambitious program, project a radically different order. Yet, the ideological point of departure is still the existing society of nations. Furthermore, in the application of such ideologies, there is a pronounced tendency to focus on a sector or region and pay little heed to the rest of the global network of international relations, and, thus, by implication, to accept the structure and processes of international society at large. Perhaps most important, in the formulation of the principles and the implementation of the programs of progressive internationalism, there is, as we shall see, a tradition for compromising by striking a balance between the ideals of the ideology and the realities of the political situation. Thus, there seems to be ground for treating both conservative and progressive internationalism as ideologies of international society (see tables 1–3).

Internationalism, it follows, is distinct from cosmopolitanism, which does not in its essence pertain to international society.[1] Proclaiming a worldwide society of individuals that overrides states, nations and groups of people, it tends to disregard all kinds of international relations and to consider only the society of human beings *en masse*. Nor is what may be called the universalism of Greens and other modern movements a form of internationalism. While cosmopolitanism transcends international society by sticking to an atomistic conception of the social cosmos, universalism does the same by taking a holistic view of the physical cosmos of mankind. Focusing on environmental dangers of general concern, it tends to go beyond most current issues of international relations in search of solutions to long-term ecological problems. However, as we shall see, elements of cosmopolitanism as well as of universalism may be found in various types of modern internationalism.

Nationalism, as the term will be used here, may be defined as the ideology of opposition to international bonding. It recognizes the existence of an international society and acknowledges its state-centric nature, but focuses on the national unit rather than the international system. Primarily concerned about sovereignty, it champions national rights, interests and values and opposes internationalist ideas, programs and manifestations that appear to threaten national independence. Since the perceptions of rights, interests and values as well as of the threats posed to them often differ, such nationalism is of several kinds. Here, as in the analysis and presentation of internationalism, a distinction will be made between conservative, liberal and socialist patterns of thought (see tables 4–6).[2]

Thus, internationalism and nationalism are opposite sets of political forces. As such, each has not only a rational but also an emotional quality. Internationalism is marked, at a minimum, by a preference for utilizing international bodies in the conduct of affairs and, more typically, by a degree of enthusiasm for the strengthening of such instrumentalities. Nationalism is generally characterized by a measure of passion in the resistance to internationalist expressions and the pursuit of national goals. If strong emotion is more in evidence in nationalism than in internationalism, as often seems to be the case, one reason may be that it is usually easier to feel deeply about something that, like the nation, is close, narrow and familiar, and thus more tangible, than about something that, like internationalist concepts of the society of nations, is distant, wide and unfamiliar, and hence more elusive. Conversely, advocating the case for international society often requires a greater input of reason than championing the claims of the nation. Thus, the coexistence and interaction of the two sets of forces may result in a balance, in which the irrational strength of nationalism checks the rationalist tendencies of internationalism.

Some of the types of thought distinguished in the following chapters, especially certain strands of socialist and liberal internationalism, may be seen as forming an ideological tradition. Their supporters, whether they developed, revived or merely espoused the ideology, were usually conscious of belonging to a long line of thinkers and actors sharing certain basic ideas and values. Other types of thought distinguished here do not presuppose such a high degree of self-consciousness, and may be described more correctly as historical trends. In their case, the element of continuity of thought may be more apparent to historians and political scientists than to their various supporters. However, whether recognized traditions or observed tendencies, the forms and types of internationalism and nationalism presented will be convenient analytical tools for tackling a vast and complex subject.

The political history of modern Europe may be seen in terms of continuous interaction between rivalling forms of internationalism and diverse kinds of nationalism. At some stages internationalist tendencies were the prevailing influences. In other periods nationalist forces were the stronger. The issue intensified in the second half of the twentieth century, when integrationist efforts provoked national reactions in both Western and Eastern Europe and separate ideological controversies ensued in the two regions. The petering out of the cold war and disappearance of the East–West division of Europe put an end to the bifurcation of ideological dispute. In the 1990s, the Western debate, which increasingly focused on the program and goals of the European Union (EU), gradually spread to most other parts of Europe.

This book is an attempt to distinguish, analyze and present the different kinds and various types of internationalism and nationalism that have played significant roles in the international politics of modern Europe, in particular during the post–Second World War (WWII) period. In each case, the origins of the ideology will be indicated, its development traced and its relationship with other strands of thought portrayed. Though the focus will be on the ideologies themselves, the roles they played in European politics will be outlined. Here, the emphasis will be on internationalist support for the establishment and development of the principal international organizations of the region and on nationalist opposition to those institutions. Such an examination of a central issue of European political thought will help to explain the contemporary state of Europe, and, perhaps, also to clarify the debate about its future.

For the purpose of identifying and examining the various patterns of thought, it will be essential to draw not only on writings of intellectuals but also on statements by prominent politicians. The reason is not merely that the study is intended to go beyond the nature of the ideas and to also touch upon their major effects on the political life of modern Europe; it is more that international politics is a field in which it is sometimes difficult to distinguish between thinkers and actors, and not always useful to separate theory from practice.

History offers many examples of writers who—like Friedrich Gentz in the nineteenth century, author of *Fragments upon the Balance of Power in Europe* and later influential secretary to the post-Napoleonic European Congresses, and Henry Kissinger in the twentieth century, author of *A World Restored. Metternich, Castlereagh and the Problems of Peace 1812–22* and later powerful secretary of state in the Nixon administration—have allowed themselves to be drawn into practical politics at the highest level. While such writers, in the role of practitioners, occasionally may draw on their scholarship, in their writings they benefit from the practical experience gained.

Conversely, many politicians have made substantial contributions to the fund of international political thought. From the old Europe of Bismarck and Gladstone to the new Europe of de Gaulle and the founders of the European Communities, there have been statesmen who have enriched the study of international politics by profound insights, wise observations or stirring visions. Thus, the following examination of internationalist and nationalist patterns of thought will draw both on relevant writings of scholars with an interest in international politics and on apposite statements by politicians gifted with sagacity and contemplative powers. (For brief background information about some of the more important but less well-known writers and politicians mentioned in the text, see the biographical glossary.)

PART I

Internationalism

Table 1 Conservative Internationalism

Type	Roots	Characteristics	Concerns and goals	Ascendancy	Exponents	Modern manifestations
Pluralist	17th century balance of power system Political realism	Pluralist notion of society of states Intergovernmental cooperation through alliances and organizations Primacy of foreign policy Low ideological self-awareness	Security through maintenance of balance of power Survival of existing states system and its units	18th and 19th centuries Post-1945 years Cold war	Castlereagh Palmerston Russell von Ranke Churchill de Gaulle	NATO and WEU OEEC/OECD (WTO and COMECON)
Solidarist	16th and 17th century Wars of Religion Christian universalism	Response to doctrinal challenge Transnational solidarity of sovereigns or governments Merging of domestic and foreign policy Ideologically explicit	Security through counterrevolutionary defense Maintenance of existing social and cultural order of Europe	Wars of Religion after Reformation Restoration after French Revolution War of Intervention after Russian Revolution Early years of European Communities	Alexander I Metternich Gentz de Casperi Adenauer	ECSC EEC

Table 2 Liberal Internationalism

Form	Roots	Characteristics	Concerns and goals	Ascendancy	Exponents	Modern manifestations
Economic	18th-century Enlightenment 19th-century international economy	Faith in free markets and harmony of economic interests	Peace through development of a society of independent nations resting on shared values, interests and institutions Prosperity through unhampered pursuit of economic interests and natural division of labor among nations	Parts of 19th century Last half of 20th century in Western Europe 1990s in world	Adam Smith Norman Angell Cobden	ECSC EEC/EC/EU BENELUX Nordic Council European Convention on HR and FF European Court of Human Rights
Political	19th-century radicalism	Doctrine of non-intervention		Parts of 19th century		
Socio-educational	19th-century national constitutionalism	Belief in democratic system and international understanding Faith in public opinion Primacy of domestic politics	Justice through protection of rights of peoples and individuals	1920s Second half of 20th century in Western Europe 1990s	Hobson Ellemann-Jensen	

Legal-organizational	Pre-1914 international constitutionalism	Faith in international law and organization Reliance on domestic analogy	20th century	
Humanitarian	19th-century radicalism	Belief in intervention for protection of individuals and minorities Doctrine of national self-determination	Late 19th century and early decades of 20th-century 1990s	J. S. Mill Mazzini Gladstone
Integrationist	20th-century federalism and confederalism	Confidence in functionalist and neo-functionalist approaches to regional cooperation	Second half of 20th-century in Western Europe	Mitrany Monnet Spinelli

Table 3   Socialist Internationalism

Type	Roots	Characteristics	Concerns and goals	Ascendancy	Exponents	Modern manifestations
Revolutionary	Industrial Revolution 19th-century socialism Russian Revolution 20th-century communism	Solidarity of working classes Revolutionary elite Doctrine of socialism in one country Communist internationalism embracing people's democracies Primacy of domestic politics and transnational links Importance of ideology	Overthrow of capitalist system, break up of class structure, withering of state and establishment of world society of equality, welfare and peace Development of socialist commonwealth of USSR and people's democracies	20th century, in USSR and post-1945 Eastern Europe and in communist parties of Western Europe	Marx Engels Lenin Stalin Kuusinen Togliatti	COMECON WTO
Reformist	Late 19th-century social democracy Pre-1914 revisionist socialism Interwar labor and social democratic politics	Transnational links among workers' parties and trade unions Recognition of usefulness of state Social reform through international organizations Belief in democratic control, big government and economic planning Primacy of domestic politics Ideological awareness	National societies of justice, equality and welfare International society of democratic, peaceful nations engaged in cooperation for progressive ends A Europe of the peoples	20th century, first in northwestern and later also in central and southern parts of Europe	Bernstein Fabian socialists Brandt Palme Delors	Nordic Council EEC/EC/EU SCANDILUX

CHAPTER 1

Conservative Internationalism

Three broad kinds of internationalism may be distinguished. Two of them, namely the liberal and the socialist, are well known and theoretically quite highly developed. The third is less developed, and barely has a name by which it is recognized. One reason for its relative obscurity is its conservative nature. In contrast with liberal and socialist internationalism, the visionary goals and progressive programs of which make them highly explicit ideologies, conservative internationalism is largely implicit, at least in its more common form. Indeed, like conservatism in national politics, it is an ideology that is sometimes held more or less unconsciously.

Despite its low profile, conservative internationalism is much older than the other two. Dating from the first centuries of the five-hundred years old European states system, it derives from a way of thinking about international politics that is conservative in the sense of focusing on what exists or has existed, rather than on what might be or ought to be. But there are two broad varieties of conservative internationalism. One, which may be traced to the operation of the balance of power in the seventeenth century, has its roots in the political realism of early European statecraft. The other, which made an early appearance in the Wars of Religion between the mid-sixteenth and mid-seventeenth centuries and reappeared after the French Revolution, springs from religious or ideological conflict in European society. It is in the former that the level of ideological consciousness is usually lower.

Origins and Nature

With the emergence of sovereign states in Europe, and the development of political interaction and diplomatic relations among them, came the balance of power. At first merely a pattern of shifting alignments, in the course of time it took on the character of a guiding rule of political interaction among several independent powers. Continual participation in the operation of the balance of power increased the understanding of the mechanics and awareness of the requirements of the system. It operated through diplomacy, alliances and war, or threat of war, and called for vigilance and prudence on behalf of its participants. It demanded a willingness to weigh the short-term against the long-term interests of the state. Above all, it presupposed an ability to recognize that several states could share an interest in opposing a preponderant power, and that all states had an interest in common in securing the continued existence of the states system and its units.

In this awareness of a shared interest in security and a common interest in survival may be seen the germs of one tradition of conservative internationalism. Having sprouted in the mid-seventeenth century, when the balance of power had reached maturity with the Peace of Westphalia, having developed in the eighteenth century, which had been the classic age of the European system of counterbalances, and having triumphed in the Napoleonic Wars, when a great power had attempted to overturn the balance and secure domination, this tradition became the major formative influence on the European Concert in the nineteenth century. Having survived the various ideological challenges of the nineteenth and early twentieth centuries, the tradition reasserted itself in the mid-twentieth century and, in a modern and more developed form, became a major force in both global and regional international politics.

The other type of conservative internationalism does not spring from the need to deal with recurrent bids for domination in the states system, but from a determination to respond collectively to intermittent doctrinal challenges in international society. It is typically manifested not so much in alliances of a number of powers as in solidarity of rulers or governments. Such solidarity usually appears in the periods of transnational tension and conflict that follow cataclysmal events of the kind described as international revolutions.[1] The first such event was the Reformation. This event was followed by generations of conflict between the conservative forces of Counter-Reformation Catholicism, championed by Spain and Austria and inspired by the papacy, and the Reforming powers, led by successive enemies of the House of Habsburg and inspired by the idea of a Protestant League. The second major event to bring doctrinal passion into European politics was the French Revolution, which introduced and exported political and social ideas that were unacceptable to the other powers. After the defeat of Napoleon, the Continental powers formed, on Russian initiative, a counterrevolutionary

Holy Alliance. Directed against radical republican ideas, it was an association of Christian monarchs for protection of the existing social order of Europe. A hundred years later the Russian Revolution brought a new ideological conflict into international politics. Challenged by communist doctrines about state and society, the Western powers fought, in the years after the revolution, an inconclusive war of intervention against Soviet Russia and all it stood for. The pattern of ideological conflict, however, was now becoming more complex.

In the battle with Bolshevik policies and communist ideology after the First World War (WWI), most of the Western powers were motivated not only by conservative but also by liberal internationalism. The next few decades saw, on one hand, a gradual spread of a democratic, reformist form of socialist internationalism and, on the other hand, a rapid rise of a fascist movement. The latter might be seen as expressing not only a particularly virulent type of nationalism but, particularly in its hostility to both revolutionary and democratic forms of Marxism and its program for reorganizing Europe along racial and hierarchical lines, also a novel and radical form of conservative internationalism of a solidarist kind. The outcome was a triangular ideological conflict between the Soviet Union and its supporters, the liberal democracies and the fascist powers. After the defeat of Germany, Italy and Japan and their allies, at the hands of an alliance, which more than anything else was a manifestation of conservative internationalism of the balance of power tradition, the central ideological conflict was again dualistic, between the Soviet Union with its allies and supporters and the Western powers. But the ideology of the West was a mixture of conservative, liberal and democratic socialist elements. Solidarist conservative internationalism, though in the Catholic Christian form it was an important influence in the setting up of the European Economic Community (EEC) in the 1950s, never became the major element in Western ideology.

In more recent years, however, it has appeared in a new form in several non-Western parts of the world. After the decline of the ideological challenge directed by Moscow and the collapse of the Soviet Union, fundamentalist movements in regions of Asia, the Middle East and Africa have emerged as actual or potential ideological opponents of the West. Based on religion and culture and transcending national boundaries, some such movements, in particular Islamic fundamentalism, seem to resemble in those respects the major manifestations of solidarist conservatism in earlier centuries of European history. If they gain influence in their regions, secure governmental power in a number of countries and maintain their passionate hostility to Western influence, a new pattern of ideological conflict might conceivably develop in the world, between the now predominantly liberal internationalism of the West and a variety of non-Western types of solidarist conservative internationalism. The current Western drive to enlarge the area where liberal values and institutions are accepted might contribute to such a development.

Since the nineteenth century, however, solidarist conservatism has most of the time been the least influential form of internationalism, whether in Europe or worldwide. Already outrivaled by liberal internationalism in the mid-nineteenth century, and challenged by communist as well as social democratic versions of socialist internationalism in early twentieth century, it has, in most of the later half of that century, been largely eclipsed by competing ideologies. The less ideological variety of conservative internationalism, however, has been a decisive influence in long periods of the history of international politics in Europe and the world, both in peace and in war. Though sometimes overshadowed by nationalism or other kinds of internationalism, it has as a rule always reasserted itself. The focus in this chapter will be on the internationalism that is associated with the balance of power and rooted in the realist tradition of international thought.

Assumptions and Concerns

Resting on pessimistic assumptions about human nature, politics and history, the old realist school of thought presents an austere picture of international society. The states system is conceived as a multiplicity of sovereign states engaged in continual interaction. Each state, in its relations with other members of the system, is seen as pursuing its own interests with whatever means it has at its disposal. Given that the interests of states are often irreconcilable, conflict is endemic and war recurrent in the system. In such conditions, security must be the overriding concern of each state. It follows that power is always at a premium, and that states constantly seek to secure their position by augmenting their own forces or forging alliances, defensive or offensive, with other powers. From Machiavelli and Hobbes to the prominent realists of the twentieth century, the principal themes of the writers of this tradition have usually been conflict and power.

As a derivative of this tradition of thought, modern conservative internationalism retains some important realist characteristics. In the first place, it is pluralist in the conception of the structure and processes of international society. Though in regional politics it may project the goal of a community, as in the case of the EEC, this is conceived as an association of states, not as a federation or a unitary state. Second, the primary concern is with the security of states. Though the concept of security may have broadened to include not only the military but also other dimensions, the basic preoccupation is with the survival of sovereign states. Third, foreign policy is separate from and prior to domestic politics. Though foreign policy and diplomatic efforts may be directed toward international organization and regional integration, the main concern is still with the high politics of great-power rivalry.

Yet, despite the realist assumptions and concerns behind this set of ideas, contemporary conservative internationalism is constructive and ameliorative, in the sense of going beyond the existing state of affairs in pursuit of a more developed international society. First, its concept of security is more complex than in most of the older realist thought. In a world of nuclear arms, it gives higher priority to international peace as a goal of diplomacy than traditional realism. Also, while acknowledging the priority of strategic and military security, it recognizes the importance of the economic dimension as well. Second, conservative internationalism is aimed at a degree of international organization. While accepting the natural conflict of interests among states, it focuses on interests that are shared and seeks accommodation through diplomacy. The ultimate goal of such diplomacy is typically some form of standing international organization, perhaps a confederation of states seeking joint security. Third, conservative internationalism may even countenance a measure of supranational decision-making in special fields. Given the interdependence of the modern world at both the global and the regional level, it may be convenient to delegate certain powers to a standing committee of representatives of the collaborating states. Since such a body would operate under the authority of the participating governments, the arrangement would not seriously compromise the basic and indispensable principle of national sovereignty. Any integration that might take place at functional levels would be simply a result of the delegation of specific powers.

The program of conservative internationalism may vary as regards the geographical scope defined, the diplomatic means employed and the political structure projected. The scope may be universal, or quasi-universal, as in the conservative strand of the ideology expressed in the establishment and activities of the United Nations (UN). It may be regional, as in the internationalism behind intergovernmental cooperation in the North Atlantic region or in Western Europe. Or it may be local, perhaps comprising just a few countries. The typical scope is regional. In such cases a regional internationalism may go hand in hand with a global realism with few internationalist qualities. This seems to have been the case in some West European thinking about international integration. Thus, part of the motivation behind the conservative internationalist drive toward a confederated Western Europe has been a desire to restore the power of Europe in global politics, by making it less dependent on the United States and more capable of holding its own in the rivalry between the superpowers.

The ways and means employed in conservative internationalist pursuits depend on the nature of the challenge. To deal with limited or transient difficulties the normal channels of diplomacy may be preferable, while a more substantial issue with some bearing on security may call for an international conference, in the tradition of the old Concert of Europe. An actual or potential threat from a hostile power may demand an alliance of the affected countries. To meet the needs arising from the interdependence of the modern world, it may be necessary to set up permanent international bodies to deal with economic or other aspects of international relations directly or indirectly related to security. In particularly exposed regions, such as Western Europe after the outbreak of the cold war, the most suitable course of action may be the formation of some kind of confederation, which is usually the most advanced form of collaboration among states advocated by conservative internationalists.

The most significant diversity, however, relates to the type of political structure projected for the more institutional forms of international cooperation. The design may be for a hegemonic order, as in some self-regarding British and French conservative internationalist ideas about the organization of Western Europe in the first decades of the European Communities. It may point toward a more oligarchic order, as in some arguments for closer bonds between two or more major powers, mostly Germany and France, in the European community of later decades. Or it may pay tribute to the principle of the equality of all participating states, as exemplified by the formal arrangement set up for the pursuit of a common West European foreign policy, known as European Political Cooperation (EPC). Such diversity of conception reflects the hierarchy of power in the international community.

Solidarist conservative internationalism, too, springs from a concern with security. But the perceived threat is not so much to the equilibrium of the states system as to the organizing principle of the international society, and takes the form of an attempt to revolutionize the structural and ideological foundations of that society. Since the means employed by the revolutionary forces may include not only war but, as in the case of the communist movements in Western Europe in the earlier period of the cold war, also subversion, the defense is likely to be directed against both external and internal enemies. Thus the nature of the challenge as well as the form of the response help to merge foreign and domestic policies. And since the revolutionary forces threaten, directly or indirectly, both a number of particular countries and international society in general, the counterrevolutionary defense tends to be mounted collectively and fought jointly, in the solidarist spirit of conservative internationalism.

The record of conservative internationalism in relation to the issue of war or peace is ambivalent. The pluralist version, as the ideology of the balance of power, has been sometimes associated with resort to war and sometimes with prevention of war. While the rules of the balance of power may call for war, its operation can also avert war. Its ultimate function has not been to maintain peace but to provide security. Yet, in the age of the cold war the central balance succeeded in protecting the security of its parties as well as averting war between the superpowers.

The role of solidarist conservative internationalism in relation to war and peace also has two aspects. While a typical organic solidarity of counter-revolutionary partners may often stifle actual and potential conflicts of interests among them, their commitment to conservative beliefs highlights the ideological and psychological dimensions of the conflict with the revolutionary camp. By focusing on the core values at issue, such internationalism is apt to impassion the central confrontation. The result may be a situation of international as well as transnational civil war, in which intense conflict not only splits the international society but also divides some of the conservative partners internally.

Though pluralist conservatism may be, on balance, rather safer than solidarist conservatism in terms of peace and war, both types of internationalism recognize war as a recurrent phenomenon of international politics and accept it as, in principle, a legitimate means of conducting foreign policy.

Developments in the Nineteenth and Early Twentieth Centuries

Most statesmen and writers of the realist tradition of thought about international politics have recognized the existence of some kind of society of nations. Usually they have seen it as a society of sovereign states, based on shared interests in maintaining order and security and held together by diplomacy and alliances or more developed forms of international organization. Even those most impressed with the salience of conflict of interests and struggle for power have sometimes gone out of their way to acknowledge elements of society. When Treitschke listed the bonds that held together his *Staatengesellschaft*, he even included war as a unifying element, because it taught nations to know and respect each other's qualities. But of course, not all of those who recognized international society were internationalists, in the ideological sense in which the term is used here.

Yet, it is not difficult to point to prominent examples in European history of people who, to a significant degree, were inspired by pluralist conservative internationalism. For more than half a century after the Napoleonic Wars, British thought about European politics was dominated by balance-of-power ideas. They were developed by statesmen and endorsed by international lawyers. Foremost among the former was Castlereagh. As a principal architect of the Vienna settlement, he was inclined to equate the European balance of power with the territorial distribution of 1815. The repose and peace of Europe, he thought, depended on the maintenance of existing boundaries. This could be achieved through the continued solidarity of the great powers, the basis of which had been prepared by the Treaty of Chaumont in 1814, largely his own work, and consolidated by the Quadruple Alliance in 1815. Such solidarity, he asserted, required a lasting British commitment. Castlereagh's idea of great-power solidarity and Continental involvement to maintain the territorial order and uphold the existing balance, which found expression in his advocacy of the congress system in the postwar period, was in the nature of pluralist internationalism.

Later statesmen gradually liberated the balance of power from the territorial settlement of 1815, at the same time following Canning in reducing British commitment to Europe. Both Palmerston and Russell saw that the idea of the balance of power transcended the reality of the established distribution of territory, and that there might be a case for sometimes letting the political principle of maintaining a balance override respect for the legal fact of the existing territorial order. For maintaining a more flexible balance of power, they relied mainly on what became known as the Concert of Europe, which was less formal than the congress system of the postwar years. Operating on an ad hoc basis, the Concert required occasional rather than regular involvement in European affairs and was thus less demanding for Britain. Though both were willing to concert their policies with other great powers when a crisis arose and the balance was at stake, Russell was more European than Palmerston. While Palmerston's commitment to Europe was qualified by his nationalist spirit, Russell was convinced that Britain "has duties to Europe as she has duties to her own people."[2] Neither, however, was as dedicated to European cooperation and Continental involvement as Castlereagh. Moreover, their internationalism was less conservative than Castlereagh's. Both of them were moved by Whig sympathies for oppressed peoples. Palmerston and, even more so, Russell allowed their attachment to the balance of power to be qualified by some enthusiasm for the idea of national liberty.

Gladstone completed the dual process of releasing the balance of power from the Vienna settlement and imbuing the conservative tradition of European involvement with liberal influences. While he upheld the principle of balance of power and the idea of a concert of powers, his preoccupation with international society took him beyond the concern with security. Ultimately intent on the advance of Christian civilization, he allowed the declining tradition of conservative internationalism to be eclipsed by the ascent of liberal internationalism.

This broad development in British thinking about balance of power and European involvement was reflected in the writings of some international lawyers in the second half of the century. While Travers Twiss, writing in the early 1860s, still tended to assume that maintaining the balance of power meant upholding the equilibrium consolidated in the Vienna treaties, Robert Phillimore, writing on the eve of the Crimean War, asserted that the former transcended the latter. And T. E. Holland, in a book published in 1885, took Gladstone's position when he argued that the role of the Concert of Europe in the Eastern Question was not only to maintain a balance of power but also to bring civilization to Turkey.[3]

Surveying the history of nineteenth-century British ideas about the balance of power, one sees a tradition of thought that in its earlier stages rested on the basis of territorial conservatism and in its later phase supported a superstructure of liberal internationalism. German thought on the subject during the same period was of a different nature and took another course. Developed mainly by north German historians, it presented the balance of power as a tendency governing the interaction of states rather than as a principle guiding foreign policy. The point of departure was again the conservative internationalism of the post-Napoleonic years, but in its dynastic as well as its territorial aspect.

In central Europe, the dynastic component of that internationalism had both religious and secular elements. The Habsburg emperors and the Prussian kings, and some of their advisers, were inclined to accept the assumption that sovereigns were servants of God who had been charged with maintaining law, government, order and peace in the Christian society of Europe. On this basis, Tsar Alexander, in 1815, had introduced the treaty of the Holy Alliance and secured the signatures of the other Continental sovereigns. Most of the conservative statesmen and publicists of the period, however, paid only lip service to the mystical insights and religious doctrines behind that treaty, or else ignored it. When they had to make a case for dynastic legitimacy, they usually based it on positive law, namely the treaties of the Vienna settlement, instead of on divine right.

The foremost exponent of the secular argument for dynastic internationalism and governmental solidarity was Metternich, who served the Habsburgs for more than fifty years. He believed that the two greatest dangers throughout the restoration period, were European war and social

anarchy. Since recent history had demonstrated that either of those calami-
ties could lead to the other, to prevent territorial aggression and to quell
revolutionary activity initially seemed equally important to him. In the
course of time, however, after France had joined the diplomatic concert of
the great powers and a series of revolutions had broken out in other parts of
Europe, he focused more on the social enemy than on the potential political
adversary. Like his adviser, Gentz, he saw the society of Europe as an organ-
ism and revolution as a disease. All revolutionary outbreaks, he believed,
could be traced to a network of secret societies and should be dealt with by
force. The remedy he proposed was a general union of European governments led by the principal powers. Such a body could counterbalance the
forces of revolution and, through judicious intervention and suppression,
prop up the existing order and stave off anarchy. Thus, Metternich's concern
with the dualistic and unstable balance of forces in the society of Europe,
came to overshadow his commitment to the multiple and consolidated
balance of power in the external relations of the states.[4]

In German thought about European politics, there was no clear division
between dynastic and territorial conservation. Tied up with each other, they
formed a complex of conservative internationalism that was solidarist, with
the dynastic strand generally the stronger of the two. Till well into the second half of the century this form of internationalism prevailed in both
Austria and Prussia. For the first generation of writers interested in the balance of power, it was difficult to resist the solidarist influences of restoration
thought.

Friedrich Gentz, secretary to the postwar European congresses, repudiated
the old balance of power that in 1806, in his *Fragments upon the Balance of
Power in Europe*, he had held up as the model to be emulated, and praised
the new system of a general union directed by the principal powers. After
1818 his political thought was motivated by fear of revolution. Like
Metternich, he saw a new balance of power in the society of Europe between
the union of sovereigns and the forces of revolution, and advocated armed
intervention and suppression of revolutionary outbreaks. Friedrich Ancillon,
cousin of Gentz and tutor to the young Frederick William IV, had also been
inspired in his earlier writings by the classical balance of power. In the postwar decade, however, he identified with the new organization of politics,
which, though apparently a deviation from the older system of counter-
forces, was in reality, he argued, its perfection. The Göttingen historian
Arnold Herrmann Ludwig Heeren, too, managed to reconcile the prerevolutionary balance of power with the postwar system. Like Gentz and Ancillon,
he embraced the doctrines of dynastic and territorial conservatism, and failed
to develop a theory of the balance of power for the nineteenth century.

Leopold von Ranke, writing in the middle decades of the century, dissociated himself from Metternichian policies and, as he put it, tried to steer a middle course between reaction and revolution. This allowed him to rise above the ideological debate of the restoration period and address himself to the great issues of the relations of states, which had dominated European history before the French Revolution. What he saw was a system with two constitutive characteristics, namely the individuality of the states and the unity of Europe. Although each nation-state was unique and independent, together they formed a society with a distinct history, common religion and shared values. In his famous essay *Die grossen Mächte*, written in 1833, Ranke surveyed the history of the states system. It was a story of incessant struggle, of new powers rising in opposition to old ones expanding, of fresh alliances springing up to defend weaker states against stronger neighbors, of Europe always maintaining its freedom and diversity in the face of successive bids for universal dominion. The most recent attempt to secure dominion, that of Revolutionary and Napoleonic France, had revived the dormant nationalities of the European peoples and invigorated the states. It was the idea of nationality that enabled Ranke to uphold the principle of state individuality against the solidarist tendencies of restoration thought, and to regenerate the balance-of-power theory. The principal powers of Europe, he observed in 1854, were like the branches of a tree, or celestial bodies "incessantly moving together side by side, sometimes in a certain conjunction and sometimes in a certain divergence from each other."[5] The heart of this system was the balance of power. By regulating the struggle among states, this mechanism sustained the duality of individuality and unity.

Ranke's system of thought gained a considerable following among his contemporaries in Prussia and successors in the *Reich*, who applied it first to European and then to world politics, making it the basis of German thinking about international politics in the half century before WWI. In the process, however, it was exposed to the influence of other ideas and attitudes, in particular those of Prussian national liberals and Hegelians. From the former came a passionate German nationalism, as expressed in the writings of Treitschke, and from the latter a set of anti-European doctrines extolling the state and vindicating its pursuit of self-interest, as evinced in the speeches and policies of Bismarck in the period before the foundation of the *Reich*. The result was a radical change in the character of German balance-of-power thought. The European outlook and pluralist internationalism reflected in Ranke's notions of cultural unity and systemic order gave way to German nationalism and political egoism. The ideas and policies of imperialist *Weltpolitik* after 1900 marked the final confluence of Rankean balance-of-power thought, German nationalism and Hegelian doctrines.[6]

The interwar period in European history was not a good time for conservative internationalism. Though there were elements of solidarist conservatism in the counterrevolutionary response of the allied powers to the establishment of the Soviet Union, and elements of a different kind of solidarist conservatism in the ideas and programs of the fascist movements and governments, the former was mixed with liberal internationalism, and the latter overshadowed by rightist nationalism. Also, pluralist conservatism was not a conspicuous part of interwar thinking about international politics. In the negotiations leading to the establishment of the League of Nations, Lloyd George and his colleagues proposed a kind of international organization much more along conservative internationalist lines than the one that was actually set up. They wanted a great-power council with both power and responsibility, which on a permanent basis could continue the European tradition of conference diplomacy, maintain the balance of power and engage in functional cooperation.[7] But the liberal internationalism of President Wilson and his colleagues prevailed. The balance of power was replaced by a system of collective security, conceived as a standing arrangement for joint defense against any potential aggressor. Though some argued that this constituted a development of the balance of power rather than marking its abolition, the new system did not enjoy the support of an effective school of conservative internationalism, and ended in miserable failure in the international crises of the 1930s. Thus, the interwar decades became mainly a period of liberal and socialist internationalism, and of nationalism.

Modern Revival

After WWII there was a revival of conservative internationalism in European political thought. Although solidarist conservatism was an element in the anticommunism of the West European nations after the outbreak of the cold war as well as in the federalist thought of the founders of the European Communities in the 1950s, the new conservatism was mainly pluralist. It appeared in both global and regional politics and, as regards the type of political structure projected for institutional cooperation, took several forms.

At the global level, pluralist conservative internationalism was evident well before the end of the war. As soon as the allied powers had gained the upper hand in the hostilities, their leaders began to make plans for the international organization of the postwar world. Roosevelt, Stalin and Churchill were determined that the special position their countries had secured in the prosecution of the war should be recognized in the structuring of the peacetime order. On the grounds that the main burden of maintaining the peace would fall on the victorious great powers, the statesmen decided to secure decisive influence for the United States, the Soviet Union, Britain, France and China, in the organization that became known as the UN. Together with the representative of China, they drew up a proposal according to which threats to international peace and security would be the responsibility of what became known as the Security Council. This body would have the power to take decisions that would bind other members of the UN. By arranging permanent membership of the Security Council for their countries, the Big Five in effect set themselves up as the oligarchs of the postwar international system. Since China, then preoccupied with its civil war, was in no position to take on global responsibilities, the oligarchy consisted in practice of the Big Four. In 1945, the two superpowers, as the United States and the Soviet Union would soon be known, and the two European great powers, Britain and France, assumed rights and duties in global international politics akin to those that the powers of the Concert of Europe had exercised much more informally and spasmodically in European politics in the nineteenth century.

The basis of the new system of peace and security was the idea of collective security. It assumed a degree of diplomatic solidarity among the principal powers, in particular between the superpowers. When the relative harmony of the war-time alliance gave way to rising tension between the Soviet Union and the Western powers, and the postwar multiple concert was succeeded by dualistic cold war, the system of collective security broke down. Within a few years it was replaced by a system of opposed alliances, which meant a return to the balance of power. One result of this development was that the scope for conservative internationalism, as expressed in intergovernmental cooperation for security purposes, was relegated from the global to the regional level.

In Western Europe, the most prominent expressions of such internationalism took the form of projects for the reorganization of Europe, which rested, explicitly or implicitly, on the idea of a hegemonic order. In 1946, in a speech in Zurich, Winston Churchill called for the formation of "a kind of United States of Europe" as a solution to the enormous political and economic problems facing the European countries after the war. But, in contrast with many others who used the same term in those years, he did not advocate a European federation, at least not one that would compromise British sovereignty. What he seems to have had in mind was more a loose association of which Britain, then still the strongest European power after the Soviet Union, would be the leader—possibly playing its part from outside the association.[8]

But the foremost example of a European statesman advocating a confederal structure built around his own state was Charles de Gaulle. In reaction to the federal drive of the Eurocrats in the 1950s and 1960s, he championed the idea of a Europe of the States. "What are the realities in Europe? What are the pillars on which it can be built? In truth they are the States.... the only entities that have the right to command and the authority to act....," he proclaimed in 1960.[9] "I repeat," he said about the Europe of the Communities at a press conference in May 1962, "that at present there is and can be no Europe other than a Europe of the States," adding with obvious reference to the schemes of the European federalists, "—except, of course, for myths, fictions and pageants...."[10] What de Gaulle had in mind for Europe was a "political union," by which he meant a community of states cooperating with each other, primarily in the fields of defense and foreign policy, while retaining their sovereignty. Governed by a personal, almost mystical, attachment to the nation-state, he rested his vision squarely on the principle of state sovereignty.

This pluralist union, obviously led by France in the west, would eventually stretch from the Atlantic to the Urals. De Gaulle, as Willy Brandt observed in his autobiography, came closer in his perceptions to a *whole* Europe than any of those who wanted to adapt rapidly and too permanently to the postwar political landscape.[11] But his ambitions for France and Europe went beyond the continent. From an early stage, he cast a united Europe in a central role in global politics. "Who can restore the balance between the two New Worlds, if not the Old World?" he asked in July 1946. "Ancient Europe, which for so many centuries has guided the universe, is in a position to provide the necessary element of moderation and understanding in the heart of a world that is tending to split in half."[12] Primarily concerned with stability, order and security, he always focused on the diplomatic and military aspects of international relations. More than most politicians of his time, he upheld the distinction between the high politics of strategy and foreign policy and the low politics of economic and social relations among states. He was a conservative internationalist in the realist tradition.

A different kind of internationalism worth considering here, is the one developed in the Soviet Union and Eastern Europe in the early decades of the cold war. As a theory about inter-socialist relations that was derived from proletarian internationalism, it naturally became known as socialist internationalism. Yet, notwithstanding its socialist origins, it had several qualities in common with pluralist conservative internationalism. In the first place, whatever else it was, it was also a theory of interstate relations. An authoritative Soviet dictionary defined socialist internationalism as "the application and the development of the principles of proletarian internationalism both in the relations between nations and nationalities who have started on the path of socialism and between sovereign socialist states."[13] While proletarian internationalism dealt only with relations among working classes and their political parties, socialist internationalism was both about such relationships and about relations between socialist states. Though the former part of socialist internationalism always was regarded as ideologically the more important, after 1948, when the people's democracies were launched on the path toward socialism, a good deal of thought was given to the latter.

Already in Stalin's last years, Soviet theorists, while continuously stressing the special quality of relations between countries with similar political and socioeconomic structures, paid tribute to the principle of state sovereignty and the norms of international law in their analysis of the interaction of socialist countries. After Stalin's death in 1953, and especially after the various crises between the Soviet Union and people's democracies in the Khrushchev years, there were further theoretical developments, with an accentuation of the tendency to pay tribute to the principles of sovereign equality and national independence. But the suppression of the "Prague spring" in 1968, led to a temporary reversal of such tendencies. The proclamation about limited sovereignty, which in the West became known as the Brezhnev doctrine, left little doubt that the international interests of the socialist commonwealth, as defined by Moscow, took precedence over the individual national interests of the constituent states. At the same time, however, there was a growing willingness to admit the possibility of conflict between socialist countries, and to explore this phenomenon theoretically. Under Gorbachev, Soviet theorists were actually encouraged to address their efforts to the interstate relations of socialist countries and in particular to tackle the problems of defining national interests and dealing with conflicts of interests between members of the socialist commonwealth.[14]

Further, socialist internationalism signified an advanced degree of cooperation among socialist states. Soviet theorists, most of the time unwilling or unable to accept the existence of serious conflict of interests between the fraternal states, continuously projected the concept of solidarity in defense of the achievements of socialism and in the struggle against imperialism. Under Brezhnev, they even paid particular attention to the coordination of the foreign policies of the socialist states.[15] The form of solidarity they were advocating, however, was quite different from the confederation of states typical of some conservative internationalist thought. Rather than a pluralist association of states set up essentially for purposes of collective security, the socialist commonwealth was a union of countries based on shared ideology and common political, economic and social structure. But, as we shall see, the practical outcome of the drive for solidarity had a good deal in common with the manifestations of conservative internationalism in Western Europe in the postwar decades. Both the military and the economic international organizations of the socialist countries were more than anything else agencies of intergovernmental cooperation.

Whatever the ultimate ideological nature of the socialist internationalism developed by the theorists and pursued by the decision-makers of the Soviet Union, it had one more thing in common with the confederal ideas championed by some British and French leaders in the postwar decades. As a blueprint for international organization, it was clearly of the hegemonic kind. From the establishment of the people's democracies to Stalin's death, the Soviet Union presented itself as not merely the only model for the economic and political development of the East European countries but also the undisputed hegemon of the bloc. Despite the formal emphasis in theoretical writings on sovereignty, full equality and mutual advantage, the program of cooperation and friendship with the Soviet Union in the name of proletarian internationalism always meant putting Soviet state interests first. With the de-Stalinization campaign under Khrushchev, there was an attempt to move from coerced union toward voluntary solidarity. In the name of socialist internationalism, the theorists began to give added prominence to the themes of higher respect for national divergences and greater equality in relations with the Soviet Union. But when Tito's Yugoslavia insisted on staying independent of the East European bloc, from which it had been expelled, and Hungary turned into a case requiring "fraternal aid," a new concern with the undermining effects of doctrinal "revisionism" led to a revived emphasis on socialist unity under Soviet leadership. Until the late 1980s, when under Gorbachev's leadership the Soviet specialists in international relations began to work seriously on the difficult concept of a "socialist partnership," the structure of the East European international system was in both theory and practice dominated by one great power.[16]

The notion of an oligarchic form of institutional cooperation has been rather less prominent in conservative thought about European politics than the idea of a hegemonic structure. When it came up, it has sometimes been as a source of anxiety rather than inspiration. The specter of a concert of Britain, France and the Federal Republic of Germany directing the EC occasionally haunted some of the lesser powers in the region, but never materialized. However, the idea of a special relationship between the governments of France and the Federal Republic, forming a kind of central axis in European politics, was advanced repeatedly and, since the days of Adenauer, at various stages pursued by the leaders of the two countries. Originally reflecting the complementary interests of the French in bolstering the security of their country and of the Germans in gaining diplomatic status and political influence, it culminated in January 1963 when Adenauer and de Gaulle signed a treaty of friendship and cooperation. Later it found fresh expression in the personal friendship and close contact between Helmut Schmidt and Giscard d'Estaing. A subsequent manifestation of the idea was the plan for the formation of a joint Franco-German armed force. Since the focus of the projected relationship was usually on intergovernmental cooperation for purposes of security, in the broader sense of the term, such ideas may be seen as expressions of conservative internationalist thought.

The ideas that projected a hegemonic order as well as those that pointed toward an oligarchic structure of the regional association of states, usually had their advocates and supporters in the countries that were cast for the principal roles in the projected system. The arguments for a more egalitarian structure were more likely to come from states that were destined for lesser parts in the system. In the Netherlands and Italy, there were occasionally negative reactions to tendencies toward the formation of a special relationship between France and the Federal Republic. Supporting an expanding cooperation of all the partners and an advancing integration of the entire region, the governments of the two countries on the whole preferred a less oligarchic structure for the EC. The conflict between the pursuit of a hegemonic or an oligarchic structure and the preference for a more egalitarian system survived the decline of conservative internationalism in the later years of the cold war and became a theme of the debate in the 1990s about the political organization and economic arrangements of the EU.

Solidarist conservative internationalism was also a feature of European thought in the later stages of WWII. It was conspicuous in some of the programs for the postwar organization of Europe, drawn up by writers and politicians of Catholic convictions. An example from Italian political debate is the platform prepared for the Christian Democratic Party entitled "Idee ricostruttive della Democrazia Cristiana," the final draft of which was written by Alcide De Gasperi in 1943. In the concluding sections, the document set out some principles for postwar international order. While all peoples should adopt the principle of national self-determination, nations should also accept limitations on their sovereignty in the interest of a wider solidarity; organs of confederation, with continental as well as intercontinental ties, should be promoted; and institutions should be set up for resolving international disputes, bringing about disarmament and discharging various other functions.[17]

At that stage of his life De Gasperi had less faith in the kind of Christian corporation that had inspired him in his youth. Under fascism, the corporatist movement had departed from its original doctrinal basis, according to which corporations were natural societies, performing social and economic functions subject to rules of justice and charity, and had identified with the fascist movement and totalitarian politics. After the reign of Mussolini it seemed important to De Gasperi to limit the role of his party to the political sector of society and leave the religious sphere to the Church. There could be no return, he saw clearly, to the promotion of a medieval kind of homogeneous society, whether in Italy or in Europe. Yet, his political thought was still inspired by his religious beliefs and Christian heritage. The European internationalism that he pursued during his years in office after the war, which pointed toward a functional integration with other Catholic countries in the first place, evinced a commitment to Christian solidarity and a faith in the transnational force of Catholicism.

In German postwar politics, the foremost conservative internationalist with solidarist inclinations was Konrad Adenauer. In the tradition of earlier times in German and European history, he saw himself as a Christian statesman. Using his God-given reason and conscience, he told an authorized biographer, he made his contribution toward "the establishment of the order willed by God even here, in this world."[18] The ideology that guided him in German and European politics was that of a Roman Catholic Rhinelander. While his Catholicism rested on the principles of the more liberal papal encyclicals, his attitude to Protestantism reflected a life-long involvement in the affairs of the Rhineland. Detesting Protestant Prussia and Berlin, he had no deep commitment to the idea of the *Reich* and no great enthusiasm for the goal of German unification. Hating Bolshevik Russia and godless communism, he identified with the West and engaged in the ideological crusade against the Soviet Union.

In West European politics Adenauer was an integrationist. As early as 1946, the year when he founded the Christian Democratic Union (CDU), he pledged himself to a united Christian Europe, declaring that he now regarded himself "primarily as a European, and only in the second place as a German."[19] Throughout his years as leader of the CDU and chancellor of the Federal Republic he was inclined to put European integration before German unification.[20] But the Europe he had in mind was a "little Europe," consisting essentially of the Federal Republic, France, Italy and the three Benelux countries (Belgium, the Netherlands, Luxemburg). It was also a Catholic Europe, initiated by Robert Schuman, Adenauer and De Gasperi and backed by the Vatican. Membership for Britain and the Scandinavian countries, all largely Protestant, was not high on Adenauer's list of priorities. It was a Europe that liberals and socialists in many countries rejected as conceived in the Carolingian tradition, promoted by a "black front" of Catholic statesmen, and supported by the conservative forces of European society.

Mainly because of the strong emphasis on integration through supranational authorities, this concept of European unity was also unacceptable to conservative internationalists of a pluralist bent. Soon after de Gaulle returned to office in Paris, the conflict between solidarist and pluralist approaches to European integration came to the forefront. Some years later when Adenauer attempted to crown his work by signing a treaty of friendship and cooperation with France, for the purpose of consolidating Franco-German reconciliation and establishing an Adenauer–de Gaulle axis in the emerging Europe, the pluralist approach had clearly superseded the solidarist way. When solidarist ideas and policies reappeared in later debates about the structure and development of the EC and the EU, it was usually in the ideological context of liberal or socialist internationalism rather than as expressions of a revived form of conservative internationalism.

Influence and Manifestations

In the 1950s, the solidarist kind of conservative internationalism was a considerable force in the international politics of Western Europe. Derived mainly from the traditional political universalism of Roman Catholicism and the revived anticommunism of the first decade of the cold war, upheld by prominent statesmen in France, West Germany, Italy and a few smaller countries, and supported by Christian Democrats and members of other integrationist political parties in the region, it manifested itself primarily in the supranational program of the European Coal and Steel Community (ECSC) and the EEC. From the outset, however, it was rivaled, and eventually eclipsed, by the other kind of conservative internationalism. During most of the cold war, conservative internationalism in Europe, as in other parts of the Western world, was largely pluralist.

At the global level, as mentioned, the principal manifestation of such internationalism in 1945 was the Security Council of the UN. When the immediate postwar state of relative diplomatic solidarity among its five permanent members gave way to strategic tension, political rivalry and ideological conflict and large parts of the world divided into opposite blocs, conservative internationalism found fresh expressions at the regional level. New organizations for international cooperation were set up, both in the East, where the Soviet Union consolidated its control of eastern and much of central Europe and received Communist China into the socialist camp, and in the West, where major powers as well as many smaller states looked to the United States for leadership.

Though each of the organizations that were established in Western Europe in the earlier years of the cold war had more than one ideological source, most of the major ones were a manifestation of conservative more than of any other kind of internationalism. Largely limited to intergovernmental cooperation, they were oriented, directly or indirectly, toward security. The motivation for the creation of one of the largest institutions, namely the Organization for European Economic Cooperation (OEEC), came from the United States.

The OEEC was originally intended as an instrument for implementing the American scheme to provide massive aid to Europe, as was first announced by General Marshall in June 1947. The organization was designed to provide information about the various national economies and to help the US government to coordinate the allocation of funds. But the American goals for Europe went beyond economic recovery. Some of the statesmen behind the Marshall Plan wanted the countries of Western Europe to integrate not only economically but also politically, and eventually form a kind of United States of Europe. The process of integration, they thought, would strengthen the free and democratic part of Europe and make it more self-reliant in the confrontation with the communist forces on the other side of the East–West division of the Continent. While they concentrated on economic means and political goals, their ultimate concern was with the military security of Western Europe and the United States.

From the beginning the Americans, in their desire for a united Europe, tried to introduce elements of supranationality in the structure of the organization. The Europeans however, the British and the French in particular but also the representatives of some smaller states, successfully opposed such integrationist pressures from across the Atlantic, and moved in different directions. As a result, the OEEC turned out to be much more modest than was intended by some of its founders. Set up in April 1948, it developed into an agency essentially for intergovernmental communication and cooperation in various economic matters. Only at the level of its technical committees did it show some functionalist tendencies. In neither the economic nor the political sphere did the organization develop significant supranational characteristics. Yet, through cooperation with the governments of the United States and Canada it became a useful bond in the unity of the West against the communist world, as did its successor the Organization for Economic Cooperation and Development (OECD) set up in 1961.

Together with the European Payments Union (EPU), set up in 1950, the OEEC and OECD represented an institutionalization of the economic and financial relations of the Western nations. This process reflected a growing recognition of the social dimension of security and a novel acceptance of the complex interdependence of modern states. Both qualities became characteristic of conservative internationalism in the second half of the twentieth century.

The most important organization created in the postwar period was the North Atlantic Treaty Organization (NATO). Though set up on North American initiative and led by the United States, with ten West European nations as founding members, joined by Greece and Turkey in 1952 and the Federal Republic in 1955, it was the foremost peace-time manifestation of conservative internationalism in modern European history. Based on the North Atlantic treaty signed in April 1949, it was also the principal security organization of the Western part of the world. Historically a response to the foreign policies and revolutionary ideology of the Soviet Union and its supporters in the first years of the cold war, which were perceived as both aggressive and subversive, the treaty and the organization were from the outset essentially defensive. In the words of the preamble of the treaty, the purpose of the signatories was "to safeguard the freedom, common heritage and civilization of their peoples, founded on the principles of democracy, individual liberty and the rule of law." NATO was conceived as an instrument of collective defense of North American and West European states, whose security interests were seen as mutually dependent. It provided intergovernmental machinery for the coordination of defense policies and collaboration of armed forces.

However, the alliance treaty also foreshadowed cooperation of a nature other than political and military. Concerned about the risk of communist subversion of Western societies, the parties declared their intentions to strengthen their free institutions, bring about a better understanding of the principles underlying those institutions, promote conditions of stability and well-being and, not least, to facilitate harmony and encourage cooperation in economic matters (article 2). Mainly in the 1950s, there was a good deal of debate about developing the economic, social and cultural potentials of the alliance, in the course of which some Canadians, Norwegians—in particular the foreign minister Halvard Lange—and others championed the idea of an Atlantic community. But nothing very substantial resulted from the debate.

In later decades, several significant developments took place in the conception of the nature and role of NATO. While at the height of the cold war the emphasis had primarily been on the military activities of the alliance, after the East–West détente in the 1960s came a new willingness to focus on diplomatic relations with the opponents. Subsequently, in particular after the decline of the cold war in the 1980s, there was a drive to make the alliance rather more European. While NATO, in the earlier decades, had rested largely on the US strategic nuclear deterrent and had involved the stationing of heavy components of US forces on European soil, now some of the European allies indicated an interest in assuming a less dependent role within the framework of the alliance. In the same period, there was also a tendency to evolve other frameworks for West European political and military cooperation. The long-standing EPC was consolidated and developed by the EC partners, the Western European Union (WEU) was revived, and some form of Franco-German military cooperation was initiated, all of which might be seen largely as expressions of conservative internationalism at regional and local levels.

More recently—after the end of the cold war, the collapse of the Soviet Union, the disappearance of the communist régimes in Eastern Europe, the outbreak of civil war in Yugoslavia and the eruption of nationalist rebellions in parts of former Soviet territory—there has been a good deal of debate about the current role and responsibilities, and the future composition and program of NATO. Whatever the outcome of that debate, the continued existence of a peace-time alliance of many nations engaged in intergovernmental cooperation for purposes of general security is organic evidence of the survival of pluralist conservative internationalism in the post–cold war world. However, the most recent engagement of NATO, the aerial bombardment of Serbia in defense of the Moslem population of Kosovo and the subsequent stationing of troops in the region, is a sign that the traditional conservative preoccupations of the alliance with the security of its members has been tempered by a revived liberal concern with human and ethnic rights in local conflicts within the European region.

Of the more exclusively European international organizations set up in the postwar decade, the most obvious manifestation of conservative internationalism was the WEU. It rested on the Brussels treaty of 17 March, 1948, a 50-years alliance between Britain, France, Belgium, the Netherlands and Luxemburg. While formally directed against a revival of German militarism, it was signed after the coup in Prague, at a time when West Europeans were more concerned with the communist threat. In 1954, the treaty was amended to include the Federal Republic and Italy in a union of states for "mutual defence and other purposes."

The principal objectives of the founding treaty were to reduce the risk of successful subversion by providing for various forms of economic, social and cultural cooperation, and to guard against armed aggression by preparing for collective military action. Article 5 was a definite commitment to collective defense, rather stronger than the corresponding article of the North Atlantic treaty. While the OEEC gradually took over the coordination of economic policies, NATO soon assumed responsibility for the planning of collective defense. Thus, in the following years the activities of the organization were mainly in the areas of social and cultural cooperation.

But after the amendment of the treaty and the entry of the two ex-enemies, the WEU took on additional functions in the field of defense. In its new form, the organization provided a solution to the problems connected with German rearmament and membership of NATO, which the aborted European Defense Community (EDC) of 1952–4 had failed to solve. With the integration of West German armed forces in the NATO structure in the years following, the WEU declined in importance and, at least as an instrument of security, eventually became dormant. In the late 1980s, however, it was revived as a convenient forum for those EC members seeking closer European cooperation in defense and security within the NATO alliance. In 1994, NATO decided that the WEU should be the European arm of the organization. By then the WEU had been expanded to include all members of the EU, except Denmark and Ireland, which in matters of defense wanted to be only observers, and many former members of the Warsaw Pact, which had the status of associate partners.

Though periodically preoccupied with social and cultural cooperation, the WEU was always basically an organization for security, which during the cold war meant internal as well as external security. While formally devoted to promoting the unity and encouraging the integration of Europe, it was never more than an agency of intergovernmental cooperation, though certain attempts were made in the earlier years to turn its Council into an executive agency that would be politically accountable to its Assembly, the former did not develop supranational elements and the latter remained purely advisory. Thus, the WEU, too, was in the pluralist mold.

The other West European organization to be considered here, the Council of Europe, eventually turned out much the same way. But in inception, as well as in its earlier activities in particular, it was a compromise between different traditions of thought about European integration. An outcome of the postwar efforts of various groups advocating what was loosely called European Union, the Council of Europe reflected the influence both of those who wanted to move toward federation and of those who were reluctant to go beyond inter-governmental cooperation. According to its Statute, signed by ten West European governments on 5 May, 1949, the aim of the Council would be "to achieve a greater unity between its members for the purpose of safeguarding and realizing the ideals and principles which are their common heritage and facilitating their economic and social progress." The means of pursuing this goal should be discussions of questions of common concern, followed by agreements and common action in economic, social, cultural, scientific, legal, administrative and other matters.

From the outset, an issue arose within the institution between the federalists, who came mainly from France, Italy and the Benelux countries, and the pluralists or functionalists, mostly British or Scandinavian. The former, inspired by the European Idea and working through the Consultative Assembly, endeavored to promote their goal of union by trying to turn the Assembly into a European parliament that would control the activities of the Committee of Ministers. But the Committee eventually rejected such proposals and maintained the intergovernmental structure of the institution. While the Assembly could make recommendations to the Committee and the latter make recommendations to the governments of member countries, the Council of Europe rested in the last resort on the principle of unanimity. The Council never developed supranational elements, but became a framework for functional activities of various kinds. However, since matters of defense from the outset were left to NATO, it did not become a security organization in the military sense of the term.

Despite the diplomatic efforts of the US government and the public campaigns of diverse movements on the Continent to push European integration beyond the limits of intergovernmental cooperation, the major agreements signed and organizations set up in the first years of the cold war were essentially pluralist. The main reason was the unwillingness of the British and sometimes the French too, to compromise their national sovereignty by accepting an element of supranationality in the new organizations. Thus, though the communist challenge to the external and internal security of the West in those years led to institutionalized intergovernmental cooperation, it did not bring about a union of Western Europe.

The international organizations that were set up in Eastern Europe during the second decade after 1945, were largely expressions of socialist internationalism. Resting on treaties that had been negotiated by communist governments, they were imbued with socialist ideology. Yet, over the years they developed characteristics that in certain respects did not make them very different from some of the Western manifestations of conservative internationalism. The two most important were the Warsaw Treaty Organization (WTO) and the Council for Mutual Economic Assistance (CMEA, also known as COMECON).

The WTO rested on the Treaty of Friendship, Cooperation and Mutual Assistance, usually called the Warsaw Pact, which the Soviet Union and seven East European countries signed in the Polish capital in 1955. Set up after the amendment of the Brussels Treaty, which paved the way for German rearmament and membership of NATO, it was obviously a security organization. While article 3 of the treaty called for joint consultation if one or more of the parties considered that a threat of armed attack had arisen, article 4 prescribed immediate assistance in the event of an armed attack on any of the parties.

Despite all ideological, political, economic and social bonds of the socialist commonwealth, the WTO was ultimately an intergovernmental agency rather than anything else. Neither legally nor politically did it develop into a supranational body. While article 5 of the Warsaw Pact called for the establishment of a unified command and article 6 for the setting up of a political consultative committee, the treaty paid respect to the principles of the independence and sovereignty of states and of nonintervention in their domestic affairs. In practice, of course, the Soviet Union dominated the alliance. But it never succeeded in making its allies accept complete integration. Operating through the bureaucratic channels, they exercised varying kinds and degrees of pressure on the hegemonic power, gradually compelling it to come to terms with their national feelings and divergent policies. Yet, though the East European security organization remained an agency for intergovernmental cooperation, it was never a pluralist association of states like the ones already established in Western Europe. In both theory and practice, the nature and activities of the WTO were conditioned by the ideological and bureaucratic bonds of the socialist commonwealth.

The CMEA was of an equally mixed character. Formed in Moscow in early 1949, in response to the challenge presented by the Marshall Plan, it comprised initially the Soviet Union, Poland, Czechoslovakia, Hungary, Rumania and Bulgaria, and from 1950 also East Germany and Albania. In the last years of Stalin, who generally preferred to exercise Soviet influence by political rather than economic means, the Council was neglected, but it was revived under Khrushchev and subsequently expanded to include also Mongolia, Cuba and Vietnam. The declared purpose of the organization was to promote the economic growth of the members by uniting and coordinating their efforts, and the basic principle once again the sovereign equality of all members. The Council should organize economic, scientific and technical cooperation, and "foster the improvement of the international socialist division of labor by coordinating national economic development plans."

Eventually the call for a socialist international division of labor within the bloc grew so strong that it came into conflict with the principle of sovereignty and equal rights. In 1960 and 1961, theorists could still stress the voluntary basis of the CMEA and describe it as "by no means...a supra-state agency with authority to intervene in the affairs of sovereign states."[21] But in 1962, Khrushchev proposed the establishment of a supranational planning authority and the drawing up of a general investment plan. The East European opposition to the proposal soon became public. While the economically developed states saw it as a threat to their national sovereignty, some of the less developed countries were concerned about the danger of being reduced to suppliers of raw materials. In 1963, the Rumanian leadership, especially alarmed by the implications of the proposal, denounced the idea of an international socialist division of labor and invoked the old principles of national sovereignty and equal rights.[22]

Though the Rumanian veto led to a shelving of the scheme, the debate continued. Soviet writers and officials, convinced that economic integration was essential for the efficiency of the WTO, pursued their goal of an ideologically correct and politically expedient division of labor among the members of the bloc. But, faced with continued opposition, in particular from the Rumanians, they gradually adopted a less coercive version of the idea and settled for something short of complete integration of the economies. Like the WTO, the CMEA did not become a supranational agency but remained more in the nature of an intergovernmental organization. Yet, like the security organization, of which it was the economic counterpart, the CMEA was in theory and practice conditioned by the ideology and structure of the bloc of socialist states.

Despite the ideological pressure from each of the superpowers—inspired, in the case of the United States, at first mainly by liberal internationalism and soon also by conservative internationalism of the anticommunist solidarist type and, in the case of the Soviet Union, by solidarist socialist internationalism—and despite the federalist campaigns and unitarian efforts within Europe itself, pluralist conservative internationalism prevailed in the shaping of the four West European organizations surveyed here. It also left its mark on the two principal East European institutions.

In the decades of the cold war, a period of neither war nor peace in which considerations of security usually enjoyed high priority, pluralist conservative internationalism maintained its influence in the region. But in the late 1980s, when East–West tension declined and attention began to shift from the regional security organizations to the UN and the EC, other kinds of internationalism gained ground. And in the 1990s, after the cold war had come to an end and before a new pattern of great-power conflict could emerge, liberal internationalism came to the forefront, and soon outdistanced both conservative and socialist internationalism.

Yet, not only the survival of NATO and the revival of the WEU but also the keenness of old and new countries in central and eastern Europe to join the developing Western security structure, or at least secure its protection, indicated that conservative internationalism was still an ideological force in the international politics of the region. As long as conflict of interests, ideas and values is a feature of relations among states, war is a recurrent phenomenon of international politics, and prudence, foresight and breadth of vision are elements of statesmanship, so long will the oldest and most basic form of internationalism continue to exist and play its part.

CHAPTER 2

Liberal Internationalism

The second kind of internationalism distinguished here is part of the liberal tradition of thought about international politics. Like liberal ideas about domestic politics, that tradition rests on confidence in the rational and moral qualities of human beings, belief in a natural harmony of collective interests and faith in progress toward more orderly social relations. Like its domestic counterpart, such liberalism has its deepest ideological roots in the doctrine of the natural rights of individuals, as advanced by the Enlightenment in the eighteenth century.

Economic and Political Forms

Resting on optimistic assumptions about human nature, politics and history, classic liberal thought about international politics features idealistic notions of the structure and processes of international society. At the heart is the idea of a society of nations that is held together by shared values, common interests and institutional bonds. Though particular policies may bring nations into conflict with each other, the deeper national interests of the peoples are believed to be in harmony when viewed rationally. Given the advance of reason and an improvement in the behavior of states, history is expected to eventually eliminate war and bring about a more peaceful and orderly world. It is a way of thinking that has allowed its adherents to focus on prosperity as their foremost social goal.

Liberal internationalism, from an early stage an element of liberal thinking about international relations rather than a later derivative from it, has generally been more developed than conservative internationalism.

Often a multifaceted phenomenon, it has appeared in a wide variety of forms. The basic one has been economic. Classic liberal internationalists tended to believe, with Adam Smith, in the virtues of an untrammeled pursuit of economic interests. If trade and manufacture could be conducted freely throughout the world, a pattern of international cooperation and peaceful competition would emerge that, they thought, would lead to a rational division of labor in global economic activities. One result of that, they expected, would be a major reduction of international conflict. Since national boundaries would no longer be economic barriers between peoples, the traditional competition for territory would cease to be a cause of war. The advantages that in the past had been associated with the enlargement of a nation's territory, whether it was done through conquest in Europe or by acquisition of colonies overseas, could now be achieved more cheaply and securely through unfettered commerce. The early liberal internationalists thought that another result of a natural pattern of economic activities and a rational division of labor among the nations of the world, would be prosperity everywhere. Maximum efficiency in the production and distribution of goods would benefit people throughout Europe and in most other parts of the world.

The ideal policy, it followed from this way of thinking, was to refrain from practically all forms of governmental interference in the economic relations of nations and to allow foreign trade to flow freely. Such a policy, early liberal internationalists believed, would not only serve the interests of both private parties and nations but also facilitate the development of international society. Even in some more advanced stages of liberal internationalism, well after it had become clear to most liberals that not all forms of governmental control or management could be dispensed with in the sphere of national affairs, there was still a tendency to rely on the "hidden hand" of *laissez-faire* in the world of international trade and finance. In the early 1990s, after the fall of communist régimes in Eastern Europe, there was a marked revival of faith in the efficacy of free market forces.

Economic internationalism has gone hand in hand with a political form of liberal internationalism. While the former has highlighted the virtues of international commerce, the latter has generally focused on the evils of governmental interference in international politics. Classic liberal internationalists, sustained by sanguine assumptions about the rationality of men and the harmony of national interests, were not inclined to preoccupy themselves with matters of external security. In their view, governmental intervention in foreign lands was in most situations as unnecessary as it was in domestic politics. Just as the activities of people within each country ought to be subjected to only a minimum of regulations, so the external relations of nations should be left to take their own natural course. The established practice of constant diplomatic meddling and occasional armed intervention rarely served any useful purpose and usually did a good deal of harm. Such governmental activities, normally conducted in the name of the balance of power or some other power-political dogma, were condemned on political as well as on legal and moral grounds. Some liberals, rather like the early socialists, even looked forward to the withering away of the state, at least in its established form.

The earlier generation of liberal internationalists included men who opposed governmental intervention against foreign countries for almost any purpose, not only when it was activated by lust for conquest or concern for the balance of power but also when it was motivated by a desire to secure the freedom of oppressed people. "I believe the progress of freedom," Richard Cobden said in the House of Commons in 1850, "depends more upon the maintenance of peace, the spread of commerce, and the diffusion of education, than upon the labors of cabinets and foreign offices."[1] Many liberals however, in Britain and elsewhere, advocated foreign intervention for liberal ends. Disturbed by the suffering of subject peoples in other parts of Europe, they called for diplomatic and military action to reform the oppressor or, more often, to liberate the oppressed. Every liberal government or people, John Stuart Mill declared as early as 1849, "has a right to assist struggling liberalism, by mediation, by money, or by arms, wherever it can prudently do so; as every despotic government, when its aid is needed or asked for, never scruples to aid despotic governments."[2] He believed that liberal institutions, his ultimate aim, presupposed national freedom.

In mid nineteenth-century France, too, there was a difference of opinion between liberals who championed the principle of nonintervention in nearly all situations and liberals who advocated intervention in the cause of freedom abroad.[3] In Italy, Mazzini, at about the same time, called for the liberation of suppressed peoples on the principle that international society ought to consist of nation states only. Such a society, he argued, would be much more harmonious than the well-known society of dynastic rivalries and interstate conflicts, because nations were naturally fraternal. During WWI the idea of liberating peoples and creating a society of nations found expression in the policy of national self-determination in Europe; and after WWII it helped to inspire the anticolonial movement in other parts of the world.

Socio-Educational and Legal-Organizational Forms

A third aspect of liberal internationalism has been socio-educational. Focusing on the individual, whose freedom and happiness usually have been their ultimate concern, liberals have generally attached much importance to education. Confident about the rationality of human beings and the perfectibility of both individual and collective behavior, they have often taught the principles of political democracy and preached the ideals of international understanding. Inclined to assume that democracy, which allows those who suffer most from war to express their opinions and influence policy, is inherently peaceable, many liberals have put their faith in educated public opinion as the ultimate protection against international aggressiveness and war. Convinced of the existence of an underlying harmony of interests among nations, they have at various stages of history promoted international understanding as a means of reaching rational resolution of conflicts and moving toward a more peaceful world. Such ways of thinking were prevalent in the 1920s, especially in Britain and some other English-speaking countries as well as among the smaller members of the League of Nations. In the 1930s, they were largely eclipsed by more power-political doctrines and programs. But in the second half of the century they reappeared in various regions of the world, including Western Europe. The collapse of communism in Eastern Europe and the end of the cold war, rapidly led to a new and much broader wave of faith in democracy and hope for international understanding.

For most of the twentieth century, however, the socio-educational aspect has been supplemented, and sometimes overshadowed, by a form of liberal internationalism that has stressed the need for developing international law and organization rather than the importance of educating individuals and peoples. Most nineteenth-century liberals tended to regard international organization as, on the whole, unnecessary and sometimes even dangerous. In dealing with international conflict, they preferred to rely on arbitration or other ad hoc processes. But many of their successors, both before and after WWI, saw the need for some more permanent machinery for managing relations and handling conflicts between states. Prominent among them were British liberals.

Motivated by fear of European war and a desire for international order, a number of British writers of the last few decades before 1914, including politicians, publicists, international lawyers and historians, most of them holding liberal views, argued the case for international organization. Some of them, for example, H. N. Brailsford and Ramsay Muir, were inspired by the record of the Concert of Europe, which they saw as representing a stage in a historical progression from total anarchy to a formal organization of international relations.[4] Their projections for the future usually amounted to an extension and a formalization of the oligarchic tendencies of nineteenth-century European politics. For some, however, the goal was rather more ambitious, namely some kind of European or world government.

Other liberal writers of that generation were more interested in the web of transnational links that had formed among peoples and groups, which to them seemed a better foundation for an organized international society than intergovernmental dealings and diplomatic coordination could ever be. The best example may be J. A. Hobson. Drawing heavily on the domestic parallel, he applied his idea of an organic unity to international relations and found that the old principle of economic and political *laissez-faire* had given way to an advancing practice of social integration. The world, in his view no longer characterized so much by the traditional political interaction of sovereign states as by the rapidly growing economic and social transactions of individuals, groups and communities, was becoming a society. The ever-increasing interdependence of the various elements of that society, he argued, created a need for some form of international organization. Rather as state governments had long since found it necessary to abandon the earlier liberal principle of nonintervention in national affairs, so the world now needed some central body to control and manage the new forces of global society. Rejecting the traditional concept of state sovereignty, he proposed a federal structure of international government in which the principles of federalism and autonomy would coexist and form a harmony of unity and diversity. Such a structure, he envisaged, would be supplemented by a number of functional agencies supported by a variety of nongovernmental bodies, many of which existed already. The experience of WWI, however, affected Hobson's ideas about international organization. His writings about the postwar world showed a greater concern with international security and peace than had been apparent in his prewar works, which had focused on justice among peoples and welfare for humanity.[5]

The ideas of those pre-1914 liberal internationalists who drew mainly on the diplomatic tradition of the Concert of Europe, and projected international organization largely in the shape of institutionalized great-power cooperation, pointed toward the League of Nations. Indeed, that body was in large part a product of liberal internationalism, especially in the form expounded by President Wilson and his followers in the Anglo-Saxon countries and some of the smaller European states. The notions of the liberal internationalists who were more impressed with the development of transnational relations and the growth of economic interdependence, and more inclined to base their schemes for international organization on the elements of nongovernmental cooperation and functional interaction, may be seen as pointing toward the theoretical and practical efforts at integration and organization that characterized Western Europe in the second half of the twentieth century. Hobson himself was, in several respects, a forerunner of the functionalists who in the middle decades of the century developed the idea of international organization through social and economic integration. However, while writers such as David Mitrany were skeptical about the idea of international government, preferring to seek social and economic reform through institutionalized functional cooperation, Hobson believed in the possibility of setting up a central body with governmental functions, and was prepared to begin exploring the legal and political dimensions of such a venture.[6]

Both strands of pre-1914 thought constituted a departure from traditional liberal internationalist thought, which from Richard Cobden in the mid-nineteenth to Norman Angell in the early twentieth century had rejected political control of economic forces. The Concert-minded as well as the more radical liberal internationalists broadly accepted the need for intergovernmental management of international relations and the importance of institutional organization of international society. They were more aware than their predecessors of the presence of conflict and the role of power in international relations. While Cobdenite liberal internationalism had represented the interests of commerce and finance in an age of relative harmony and stability, the revised internationalism of the later writers reflected an increasing concern with peace and security in a period of growing conflict in the world and rising tension in Europe.

For the liberals, in Britain and elsewhere, who believed in international government, the establishment of the League of Nations after WWI was a big step toward the goal. In the 1920s, they could devote much of their energy and time to reinforcing the machinery for peace, whether by covering loopholes in the Covenant of the League or by inventing other legalistic means of preventing future wars, as well as to strengthening the social and ideological bases of the new institution by trying to educate people in liberal democracy and international understanding.[7] But the disappointing performance of the League in the major international crises of the 1930s, in a situation of rapidly rising international tension and growing ideological conflict, offered little encouragement to further such endeavors. It was only in the later years of WWII that history again provided a major impetus to experiments in quasi-universal political organization. The outcome was the UN. But liberal hopes for the new institution of world politics were soon checked by the East–West division of the great powers and the emergence of the cold war. After the middle of the century, liberal efforts at international organization took largely regional or local forms, producing some of their most substantial results in Western Europe.

As in the first phase of liberal thought about international organization, there were two broad, and not always clearly distinguishable, approaches to the organization of Western Europe in the postwar decades. One, which might be called the constitutionalist approach, was more direct and essentially political and juridical, while the other, labeled evolutionist, was more indirect and mainly economic and social. But, while the constitutionalists had predominated in the first decades of the century, the evolutionists were on the whole preponderant in the later period. The strongest element in the evolutionist pattern of thought was functionalism. With its program of social and economic reform through transnational cooperation, functionalism had a broad political appeal. Going beyond the old liberal goal of national prosperity and aiming specifically at welfare for the peoples, it could inspire not only some liberals, in particular radical liberals, but also more reformist socialists. The principal effects of functionalism on liberal internationalism were to strengthen its social dimension and broaden its political appeal.

Humanitarian Form

The development of the organizational form of liberal internationalism, especially in its more socialized version, ultimately reflected the advancing economic and technological interdependence of nations in the twentieth century. The growing recognition of such interdependence was more recently followed by a new awareness among liberals of an international community of shared values and collective responsibilities. The result was a revival and development of a distinctly moral form of internationalism that had enjoyed some prominence in liberal thought in the later part of the nineteenth century—particularly in Britain, then the most liberal of the European great powers—but later had gone into decline, and eventually given way to other forms of liberal internationalism.

Before liberal internationalism in pre-1914 Britain became distinctly organizational, it often took a more humanitarian form. Already in the middle of the nineteenth century, John Stuart Mill could argue that a new principle of international law had been established, according to which other countries had a right to step in and impose reasonable terms of accommodation whenever two countries, or two parts of the same country, were engaged in war, and the war either continued long undecided or threatened to be decided in a way involving consequences repugnant to humanity or to the general interest. It was too late in the day, he insisted, "to tell us that nations may not forcibly interfere with one another for the sole purpose of stopping mischief and benefiting humanity."[8]

About thirty years later, during the crisis in the Eastern Question in the late 1870s, Gladstone took up the humanitarian case, linking it to the principles of international law and the practice of the Concert of Europe. Inspired by classical literature and guided by the doctrines of Christianity, he challenged the enemies of religion, reason, justice and humanity and made a stand for morality in European politics. History, he believed, was on his side in the great struggle: "... there is going on a profound mysterious movement, that, whether we will or not, is bringing the nations of the civilized world, as well as the uncivilized, morally as well as physically nearer to one another, and making them more and more responsible before God for one another's welfare."[9] This advance in international morality, he thought, was reflected in the development of the law of nations and manifested in the evolving functions of the Concert of Europe. His passion was roused by the sufferings of Christian subjects of the Ottoman Empire, and he demanded collective measures by the great powers to put an end to the atrocities. Such measures, he insisted, during the last two years before the Congress of Berlin, should include not only the traditional measure of exacting reform from the Porte but should also be novel and bring about self-government for the disturbed provinces.

A later generation of British Liberals, incensed by the Turkish treatment of Armenians and inspired by the Cretan struggle for freedom, upheld the humanitarian strand of liberal internationalism. In the 1890s, both Lord Rosebery and Joseph Chamberlain pinned their faith on the Concert of Europe as the instrument for reform of Turkey. Sir Edward Grey looked to the Concert for action almost till the eve of WWI, to save the Christians of Armenia and Crete in 1897 and 1898, to bring about Macedonian reform in 1908, and to organize a comprehensive reform of Turkish government in 1913. While Mill had gone as far as countenancing liberation of oppressed peoples and Gladstone more cautiously had argued for their self-government, the prewar generation of Liberals were inclined to confine themselves to calling for reform of the oppressor, whether through concerted diplomatic pressure or through coercion.[10]

Both the organizational and the humanitarian strand of liberal internationalism came to fruition in the decade after WWI, the former through the establishment and activities of the League of Nations and the latter by way of the emergence and development of new states in parts of Europe, which for long had been subjected to Ottoman, Habsburg or Russian sovereignty and thus exposed to suppressions of various kinds and degrees. The following period of European history, marked by diplomatic crises and prolonged war, was not a good time for liberal internationalism of any kind. But in the second half of the century such internationalism reasserted itself in various forms. While organizational internationalism was manifested regionally in the politics of Western Europe in the decades of East–West tension, humanitarian internationalism came to the forefront after the end of the cold war. The collapse of the Soviet Union put an end to the division of Europe into spheres of superpower influence and made it possible for Western governments to take a more active interest in the affairs of states formerly under communist rule. Moreover, the revolutions, rebellions and wars in some of these countries in the 1990s, particularly in the former Yugoslavia, created a need for humanitarian intervention. Thus, many European liberals, inspired by a revived notion of international responsibility, grew more inclined to advocate collective aid for countries in turmoil and, in extreme cases, joint intervention to curb hostilities and deal with acts of atrocity.

The willingness of such liberals to sometimes set aside both the legal doctrine of domestic jurisdiction and the political principle of nonintervention in order to defend the rights and safety of needy groups and individuals in other countries was not the only distinguishing feature of the new form of humanitarian internationalism. In the later decades of the century it was complemented by a growing inclination to go beyond national boundaries and parochial concerns for the sake of protecting the common good of the human species against threats to the environment. Reflecting concerns that ranged from the rights of particular individuals to the interests of humanity in general, humanitarian internationalism broadened the conventional transnational conception of international society, partly by stressing the cosmopolitan element of liberal thought and partly by giving such thought a new universalist dimension. Embracing both the social and the physical cosmos of mankind, the revived humanitarian strand of thought increased the complexity of modern liberal internationalism. The development of both the organizational and the humanitarian strand in the second half of the twentieth century, ultimately reflected the multidimensional and ever-increasing interdependence of countries in both Europe and the world.

Both more developed and more involved than its conservative counterpart, liberal internationalism is also profoundly different in most other respects. Historically it has been motivated by an optimistic faith in international harmony and a confident expectation of general progress, rather than by a prudent preoccupation with survival and security in conditions of rivalry and conflict. At its heart is still the idea of an international society that is made up not so much of states as of nations or peoples and, especially in its socio-educational and moral-humanitarian forms, even of individuals. Its overriding concern is not with the collective defense of shared national interests, or even the joint management of international interdependence, but with the prosperity of nations and, ultimately, the rights of individuals. Its political program is not so much a pragmatic response to concrete challenges and immediate difficulties as a design for reform of international politics and development of international society. This design goes beyond intergovernmental cooperation, and points toward advancing integration at several levels of international interaction: economic, political, social, institutional and moral. Foreign policy, in the liberal internationalist view, is not separate from and superior to domestic politics but rather an extension of it, both of them resting ultimately on notions of human rights and ideals of the good life.

Many of the differences between conservative and liberal internationalism are connected with their different social origins. While conservative internationalism sprang from a tradition of politics developed by aristocratic statesmen schooled in the ways of the old Europe of dynastic rivalries and territorial sovereignty, liberal internationalism was largely the creation of the middle classes that emerged in Western Europe in the last two centuries and mostly gained their political experience within their own countries. Reflecting the interests, values and convictions of merchants, manufacturers, intellectuals, lawyers and other professionals, it was in both its goals and its means the philosophy of people who in their conception of the world tended to be guided by the notion of the domestic analogy, according to which the structure and processes of the world, or at least their own geographical region, should become more analogous to those of domestic society.[11] Liberal internationalism became particularly influential in Britain and among the smaller countries in northwestern Europe, where democracy first struck roots.

Integrationist Forms

In the decades after WWII, liberal internationalism became a powerful ideological influence in large parts of the world. Taking several forms, it made a mark at all levels of international society. In global, or quasi-global, affairs the prevalence of the ideology reflected the powerful role of the English-speaking powers in the later years of the war and the following period. As part of their wartime thinking about the postwar order of the world, the

British and American governments had committed themselves to the creation of a liberal international economy. Their plans had included a stabilization of the rates of currency exchange and a reduction of tariffs and other barriers to free trade. A conference of the representatives of some 44 governments, held at Bretton Woods in New Hampshire in July 1944, had dealt with the financial side of the new order. The principal result of the meeting had been the establishment, in December the following year, of the International Bank for Reconstruction and Development (IBRD) and the International Monetary Fund (IMF). Later the United Nations Economic and Social Council (UNESCO) had called a conference with the aim of abolishing quotas and reducing tariffs, the outcome of which had been the General Agreement on Tariffs and Trade (GATT) of October 1947. As an instrument for liberalizing world trade, that treaty was to prove more efficient than any other postwar agreement.

In postwar Europe, liberal internationalism was more in evidence at local levels than in the broader region. In relations among Belgium, the Netherlands and Luxembourg, it was an important element in the ideas and attitudes that in 1948 led to the formation of BENELUX, which started as a customs union and evolved into a broader economic union. After the war the debate among the five Nordic countries, too, was influenced by liberal internationalism. Though they did not succeed in reaching their goal, the governments developed far-reaching plans for abolishing all internal Nordic tariffs and forming a customs union. Furthermore, liberal internationalism was part of the ideological background to the discussions and negotiations that in 1952 led to the establishment of the Nordic Council, which became the institutional framework for a much broader form of Nordic cooperation.

But it was in the discussions and preparations that led to the establishment of the ECSC in 1952 and the founding of the EEC in 1957 that liberal internationalist ideas played their most important role in European postwar politics. Liberal economic principles were part of the ideological foundation of both institutions. The men who set up the ECSC believed in transnational integration as the best way to efficient production. But their sectoral approach to integration—also characteristic of those who championed Euroatom in those years—was inadequate for some of the more far-sighted European leaders. The latter wanted a much broader economic integration, which would start with a customs union and move toward full economic union. Their idea of achieving economic and social progress by reducing the obstacles to free trade was enshrined in the Treaty of Rome. Thus, the brand of liberal internationalism already expressed in BENELUX was applied to a much wider geographical area.

The subsequent debate about the evolution of the EC led to further development of liberal internationalist thought. It became closely tied up with integration theory. In the process, it sometimes merged with functionalism, which earlier in the century had been an element of some liberal internationalist writings and subsequently had acquired an identity of its own, as a theory and policy of sectoral, local or regional integration. Later liberal internationalism also became associated with the branch of integration theory known as neo-functionalism.

In the great confluence of ideas that gave rise to the establishment and shaped the development of the EC, both functionalism and neo-functionalism acquired a rather hybrid character. Sometimes the former became linked with goals traditionally associated more with conservative internationalism, such as peace and security. The latter often became tied up with socialist goals, mainly public welfare through administrative control. But in their commitment to functional interaction as the way to some form and degree of regional integration, both functionalism and neo-functionalism belonged to the liberal tradition of internationalism.

Functionalism

Like traditional liberal thought about international relations, European functionalism concentrated, in the first place, on the nonpolitical aspects of international society. It highlighted the growing economic, social and environmental bonds among peoples and nations as well as the advancing technology that was revolutionizing their industries, communications and ways of interacting with each other. In a true liberal spirit, the functionalists saw such developments as strong incentives to transnational cooperation and international organization, rather than as possible sources of friction and conflict. For many of them, the new forces pointed toward a degree of political unity, initially at local or regional levels but eventually perhaps much more widely. Their ultimate goals seemed to be a transition from international to world politics, and the emergence of a global society made up of functionally interacting units. That kind of functionalism, it might be said, represented a marriage between the facts of modern interdependence and the ideas of traditional liberal internationalism.

Again like liberal internationalism, European functionalism focused not only on the influence of various forces and developments in the international system but also on the role of the individuals who made up the units of that system. Here, as in classical liberal thought, the basic assumption was that human beings were rational enough to let their economic and social needs govern their collective behavior. Inclined by nature to support institutions and policies most likely to satisfy their basic requirements, men and women, functionalists argued, went through a learning process when involved in transnational activities and international cooperation. As the results of functional collaboration became apparent to them, they would call for more programs and welcome new organizations. Eventually, it was thought, they would develop new loyalties, and come to accept institutions that were not based on the old national territorial boundaries but defined rather in terms of functional role in a wider community.

At both the systemic and the individual level of analysis, functionalism belittled the importance of political conflict between states. The exponents of the theory tended to assume that advancing cooperation at nonpolitical levels and growing integration in functional spheres would gradually overcome international conflict of the traditional power-political kind. The territorial state itself, they thought, would eventually come to seem obsolete. That institution, which many liberal internationalists of earlier periods of European history had seen as a source of mischievous intervention in foreign affairs and an obstacle to the peaceful pursuits of peoples and which the functionalists of the twentieth century tended to view as an impediment to international organization and European integration, would have to give way, they believed, to the transnational forces of the modern world and the rationality of man. Thus, in the last analysis, the pursuit of prosperity and welfare would eclipse the concern with power and security. As an ideology of integration, functionalism became particularly influential in the early years of the EC, when it merged with liberal and other forms of internationalism.

Good material for a study of the merging of liberal internationalism with functionalism in integrationist thought can be found in the writings of Jean Monnet. Though widely regarded as the foremost functionalist statesman of his age, Monnet was always more than that. As early as the mid-1940s, long before the planning of the ECSC, he was a federalist. In the last years of the World War, he argued for the setting up of a postwar order in which the European countries would form a federation, "a European entity," and become a single economic unit.[12] On the occasion of the signing of the convention of the OEEC in Paris in 1948, he argued instead for the establishment of a "federation of the West."[13] Later, when submitting a draft paper about the role of the projected High Authority of the ECSC, he explained that the point was to lay "the concrete foundations of a Federation of Europe."[14] Several years later, when announcing his plans to retire from the presidency of the High Authority, he declared that "what is being achieved in our six countries for coal and steel must be continued until it culminates in the United States of Europe."[15] Though inspired by federalist goals, Monnet was not attracted by the various draft constitutions championed by ardent federalists in the postwar decades. Rejecting their direct approach, he devoted himself to the gradual way of the functionalists, which he found "more pragmatic and more concrete." His program, and the arguments he advanced in its support, had pronounced liberal elements.

In the last years of WWII as well as in the long period of European reconstruction, Monnet's overriding concern was to bring the age of competing nationalisms, with all its conflict and bloodshed, to an end and secure lasting peace in Europe. He focused his efforts on the relationship between France and Germany, first with a view to preventing a revival of economic and political conflict between those long-standing enemies, and subsequently, as the East–West conflict in Europe and the world intensified, in the hope of stopping Germany from becoming the prize of a third world war. Convinced that the only secure foundation for future peace would be an integration of the economies of potential enemies, he thought that the first step should be the merging of the heavy industries of West Germany and France. Coal and steel, in the production of which the Germans in the long run would be superior to the French, had in the past been the raw materials for warfare and, it could then be assumed, would be so in the future as well. Other European countries wishing to participate should be included in the merging of these national industries. Subsequently, he argued, the integration should be deepened to include the entire economic systems of the partners, and widened to take in other countries, of which he regarded Britain as the most important. The result, in political terms, would be a European union of states and, in economic terms, a great internal market with tariffs cut to a minimum. The ultimate basis for such an integration of Europe, or large parts of it, would be the interests that all people shared in raising their standard of living and avoiding major war. Essentially a development of the classical liberal doctrine of peace through free trade and economic prosperity, Monnet's argument for functional integration rested on the principle of a regional harmonization of economic interests. What he projected, he said, was a system "in which, to everyone's advantage, the idea of the common interest would replace that of the national interest."[16]

The argument also assumed a rather high degree of rationality on the part of the peoples involved in the process of integration. On the whole, Monnet believed, people were inclined, or at least could be persuaded, to act in their common material interest provided they were able to perceive that interest. Hence a very important part of the process of European integration was to educate people. "Changing the way people thought" was the psychological counterpart of the material side of integration. It was a dual process, the foremost result of which was the new institutions that were being set up. And these institutions themselves would play an important part both in shaping Europe and in educating the Europeans. They would not only accumulate the collective experience of people but also transform the social behavior of men and women. "Nothing is possible without men: nothing is lasting without institutions" was Monnet's own summary of his faith in men and institutions.[17] Underlying his whole philosophy of politics was a strong belief in continual progress, not as a predetermined outcome of an inevitable historical process but as the result of purposeful political efforts.

The method he championed, a gradual merging of economies at the functional level and a slow fusion of power on the governmental plane, represented a radical departure from the traditional intergovernmental form of international cooperation. He was convinced that such cooperation, usually managed or controlled by several governments and limited or conditioned by actual or potential rivalry among sovereign states, could not meet the problems of contemporary Europe. Only a blending of the material interests of the European peoples and the establishment of an administrative network of supranational management could overcome the inherent conflict among the states and secure the future of Europe. While economic integration of peoples would gradually eclipse political rivalry among governments, a growth of functional régimes would undermine and eventually do away with the state in its traditional form. Rather as provinces had united into nations, so the nations of Europe, Monnet thought, could unite as a community with common rules and institutions. Such a community, he suggested, might serve as an example for other conflict areas of international politics. The Arab–Israeli issue, for example, might be overcome, in the course of time, through the establishment of a community of the nations of that region. Thus, the Community of Europe, he could declare in the mid-1970s, was only "a stage on the way to the organized world of tomorrow."[18]

The picture of an organized world of regional communities conjured up by that sentence, with which Monnet concluded his volume of memoirs, was an ideal in the liberal internationalist mold. But there had always been other, rather more realist, elements in his argumentation for a united Europe. In the later part of WWII, when he projected the formation of a "European entity" that would constitute a single economic unit, he gave as one of his reasons the peculiar geopolitical situation of France. While the British, the Americans and the Russians had worlds of their own into which they could withdraw periodically, the French were bound up in Europe and could never escape. Hence the future life of France depended on finding a solution to the

European problem.[19] In preparing his scheme for the postwar organization of Europe, he was wondering whether Britain could be brought in, so that Germany did not once again become preponderant in the European system.

In the postwar decades, Monnet's power-political considerations did not always focus on the situation of France in Europe but also increasingly on the role of Europe in the world. After the introduction of the Marshall Plan and the establishment of the OEEC, his motivation for seeking a federal solution appeared to be a growing concern about European dependence on American credit and strength as much as a preoccupation with the Soviet threat.[20] By turning the industries of war into a common asset, he told Adenauer after the presentation of the Schuman Plan, Europe would rediscover the leading role it used to play in the world.[21] The scale of modern technology, and the size of America and Russia today or of China and India tomorrow, he asserted four years later, called for a union of the European peoples.[22] In answer to de Gaulle's caustic comments on the efforts to unite Europe, Monnet declared in 1962 that "only through the economic and political unification of Europe, including the United Kingdom, and the establishment of a partnership of equals between Europe and the United States can the West be strengthened and the conditions created for peace between East and West."[23] Thus, he came to present the unification of Europe and equality with the United States as steps toward reconciliation between East and West.

Though the motivations behind Monnet's communitarian approach to regional and global politics may have been diverse, liberal influences were conspicuous in his functionalist commitment to European integration. They were evident in the means he advocated, namely economic integration and institutional organization, as well as in the assumptions he made, especially of a fundamental harmony of interests and of the rationality of people. However, like most writers and politicians of his time who advocated European integration, he did not share the love of the nation-state characteristic of so many liberal internationalists of earlier generations. Nation-states and international society were no longer the end product of liberal endeavor but the starting point of an evolution toward a European community.

Neo-Functionalism

The neo-functionalist approach to European integration may be seen as both a reaction to and a development of the functionalism of the postwar decades. Initially inspired by the emergence and establishment of the EEC, in turn it helped to stimulate and guide the further development of the Community, to the point where it could be described as an unofficial ideology of the EC. Like the functionalist integrationists, neo-functionalists saw integration as rooted in various social and economic forces. But neither the process itself nor its results were seen in quite the same way. According to neo-functionalists, it was not so much through the direct incentives to transnational interaction and international cooperation presented by certain social, economic and technological forces and developments that integration came about, as by way of the intermediary effect of the various entities that gave political expression to such forces and developments. In their cautiously competitive interaction, these entities—which included corporations, pressure groups, political parties or movements, government agencies and international institutions—developed, shaped and strengthened the organizations through which they conducted their business. The ongoing reconciliation of interests among the various parties helped to enlarge the scope and enhance the authority of those organizations. The outcome of the process, it was argued, was a community, distinguished by a mixture of collective national and supranational decision-making. If, in the longer run, there was a continual growth of supranational decision-making and integrated administration, the traditional distinctions between politics and administration and between international and domestic politics would become even more blurred. Thus, the entire development pointed toward some kind of federal structure.[24]

While neo-functionalist, like functionalist, analysis of European integration had pronounced elements of liberal internationalism, the form of such internationalism was not exactly the same. In functionalism, which brought the socio-economic forces of the international system as well as the rational and moral qualities of human beings into the analysis, the prevailing forms were those that here have been called the economic and the socio-educational versions of internationalism. In neo-functionalism, which focused more exclusively on structural evolution in the sphere of political–administrative interaction, the principal liberal internationalist influence appeared to be of the legal-organizational kind. The primary concern was with the organized interaction of governments and political elites. It was mainly in the analysis of the process of integration that the liberal internationalist element was of some influence. In the projection of the goal of that process, conveyed largely through the emphasis on the emergence of supranational régimes, the dominant element was that of federalism. As regards both the process and the goal of integration, neo-functionalism was a Eurocratic theory.

One of the foremost exponents of the neo-functionalist approach to European integration was Altiero Spinelli, who was a European Commissioner during 1970–6 and subsequently a member of the European Parliament. With a background in antifascist resistance, he was as convinced as Monnet of the evils of nationalism, the obsolescence of the state and the need for lasting peace in Europe. He also agreed that the way ahead was through new institutions and that the goal was a European federation. But he disagreed with Monnet and other functionalists about the manner in which these institutions should be established and the goal achieved. The early functionalists had had unlimited faith in the integrative capacity of the administrations they had set up, he complained, and had failed to see the need for active measures to organize political power in the European sphere. The result of their efforts at unification had been the creation of a new body, namely the EC, but it was a body without a head.[25] "Monnet," Spinelli said toward the end of his life, "has the great merit of having built Europe and the great responsibility to have built it badly."[26]

In order to continue the work of the functionalists, Spinelli pleaded for a more constitutional approach. Intending to build on the "Europe of supranational offices" that had been erected in the 1950s and early 1960s, he advocated a program of major institutional reform and consolidation. For the purpose of strengthening the political center of the new Europe, it was necessary, he argued, to subordinate the supranational administrations to some form of federal government. In particular, he wanted to increase the powers of the Commission and the Parliament, and thus strengthen both the political and the democratic control of the emerging European union. Rather than wait for slow organic growth through functional interaction, he preferred the course of decisive intervention at opportune stages. In the early 1980s, he launched a major initiative in the European Parliament that eventually led to the Single European Act of 1985. The central idea of that act was to move toward a European union by formalizing the rules and practices associated with the EPC, expediting the process of setting up a single market and strengthening the EC institutions.

As a federalist, Spinelli was in the democratic tradition of the first postwar years. Like most of the former members of the Democratic Left in the antifascist resistance movements who after the war had campaigned for a federal organization of Europe, he believed that the new institutions would derive their legitimacy from consent expressed directly by the citizens of Europe and should exercise their powers directly upon those citizens, with as little interference as possible from the member states.[27] He was critical of the more conservative liberals of the postwar decades who had played a role in the efforts to unify Europe. Though the constitutional principles and economic doctrines of old-fashioned liberalism had enabled them at times to formulate a European concept of extraordinary clarity and consistency and had allowed them to readily accept the Common Market, their historical love for the nation-state, he pointed out, had led them to be swayed by nationalist feelings when the needs of the EC clashed with national interests.[28] Spinelli, while accepting the free-market philosophy of liberalism and recognizing the integrative dynamics of functionalism, focused on the task of overcoming the institutions of the state and the structure of the international system in Western Europe. Concerned as much with processes as with goals and values, he was a radical in European politics.

While the functionalists were more influential in the drive for European integration in the 1950s and early 1960s, the neo-functionalists left a stronger mark on the debate in the following period, until the slow-down in the development of the EC in the 1970s discouraged their efforts. The successful negotiation of the Single European Act in the mid-1980s, however, strengthened the hand of the neo-functionalists and revived their influence. To the extent that the two strands of functionalism were influenced by liberal ideas and values, they helped to uphold the liberal internationalist tradition in the West European debate.

In the half century after WWII, this tradition enjoyed wide support in most noncommunist countries of Europe. At the governmental level, its appeal was apparently particularly strong among the smaller countries. The three governments that in 1948 set up BENELUX, were largely motivated by liberal ideas. Whatever their party-political affiliations, so were the five Nordic governments that in the same period pursued the idea of a customs union and in 1952 set up the Nordic Council. After the collapse of communist government and the introduction of market economies in Eastern Europe the governments of the countries that sought an early membership of the EC, namely Poland, the Czech Republic and Hungary, became rapidly converted to an internationalism with a pronounced liberal orientation.

Among the political parties, liberal internationalism drew support not only from the Liberals, who were generally enthusiastic about the Common Market, but also from a variety of other parties that welcomed the economic developments and some of the institutional arrangements in Western Europe, such as the new Christian Democrats in the EC and the Conservatives inside or outside the various international organizations. In West European society at large, the groups representing the interests of commerce, and much of industry as well, were also guided largely by liberal internationalist doctrines and values. Most young people of the "interrail generation" seemed to be inspired by similar ideas. Finally, within the various European institutions, many though not all the bureaucrats were motivated by liberal internationalism, whether moderate or radical. Generally speaking, liberal internationalism enjoyed broader support than conservative internationalism.

Influence and Manifestations

Though, as we have seen, not always the principal source of ideological inspiration, liberal internationalism left a mark on most of the international organizations that emerged in Western Europe in the first years of the cold war. The OEEC, as well as its successor the OECD, owed much to liberal influences, which came from several sources. To the extent that the former organization originally came about in response to American attempts to make the European countries integrate economically and politically and form a United States of Europe, it was largely conceived in the messianic spirit of American liberalism. However, European resistance to integrationist pressures from the United States resulted in a program rather less ambitious than what the Americans had in mind. When the founding agreements of both the OEEC and the OECD nevertheless contained liberal internationalist elements, it was mainly because of the influence of the European governments themselves. The Convention of the OECD, defining its aims as economic growth, in the member states as well as in developing countries, and expansion of world trade, set out its principles as promoting the efficient use and development of economic resources and endeavoring to reduce or abolish obstacles to the exchange of goods, services and payments and to the flow of capital. Moreover, both organizations developed rudimentary functionalist characteristics in the course of their activities. But despite the varying emphasis on the goal of economic prosperity, the principle of free markets and the practice of functional integration, all such elements of a liberal internationalist nature were ultimately means of pursuing the end of security. They were seen as essentially ways of strengthening the social fabric of free, democratic countries in a prolonged struggle with the emerging bloc of communist countries. Thus, OEEC/OECD should be seen more as a manifestation of conservative than of liberal internationalism.

This, of course, was also true of the other important international organization set up with North American participation and under US leadership in those years. The North Atlantic Treaty contained several references to the principles of democracy, individual liberty and the rule of law, to the pursuit of stability and well being in the North Atlantic area and to the encouragement of economic collaboration between the members, which provided a basis for some subsequent debate about developing the economic, social and cultural potentials of the alliance and embodying the idea of an Atlantic community. But NATO always remained a security organization. When its members, in the early years of the alliance, complemented their efforts in the military field with a certain amount of attention to economic developments, social conditions and cultural relations, it was largely because they saw the communist powers as presenting a dual threat, of subversion as well as aggression.

The WEU, too, was conceived as a security organization. Though the Brussels Treaty, on which it rested, provided for various forms of economic, social and cultural cooperation and integration, the objective was to guard against the risk of successful subversion by the communist governments and their sympathizers, rather than simply promote the prosperity of Western Europe. But once most of the economic parts of the projected activities had been taken over by OEEC and the military parts by NATO, WEU was left with little more than social and cultural relations to occupy itself. The spirit with which the signatories sought collaboration in these fields may have been animated largely by liberal internationalism.

The influence of such internationalism was rather more apparent, however, in the origins and early development of the Council of Europe. That body, set up in the first stage of the cold war and designed to defend the ideals and principles of the West European countries and to facilitate their economic and social progress but not allowed to evolve beyond its intergovernmental structure, has been considered under the heading of conservative internationalism of the pluralist kind. It was ultimately concerned with security, though of the political, social and economic rather than of the military kind. But, as we have seen, in both inception and development it was also influenced by strands of thought about European integration not usually germane to that form of internationalism. One was federalism, the influence of which was apparent in the definition of the goal of greater unity among the members, in the emphasis on the means of common action in economic, social, cultural, scientific, legal, administrative and other matters and, not least, in the attempt to turn the Consultative Assembly into a European parliament with controlling powers over the Committee of Ministers. Another formative influence was that of the functionalists, who helped to define the goals and means of the Council and establish it as a framework for a variety of functional activities. Though the federalists and the functionalists sometimes pulled in different directions in matters of integration, their programs for the Council of Europe contained elements of liberal internationalism.

More clear-cut early examples of institutional manifestation of this kind of internationalism appeared at the local level of West European politics.

One of the first was BENELUX, which after its formation in 1948 gradually evolved into a deeper economic union. In contrast with the other associations of states for economic cooperation considered here, it was primarily a case of economic integration for purposes of prosperity, rather than of security. Another example was the Nordic Council, which Denmark, Iceland, Norway and Sweden set up in 1952 and that Finland joined three years later. It was a forum in which parliamentary representatives of the five countries could seek coordination and cooperation in a wide range of fields and make recommendations. After 1962 this work was regulated by the Treaty of Helsinki, which provided for cooperation in the juridical, cultural, social and economic areas as well as in matters relating to transport and communication and the protection of the environment. In 1971, a Nordic Council of Ministers, representing the five governments, was set up with powers to submit proposals and implement decisions. Though matters of foreign policy were discussed, the traditional concerns of the two councils were with prosperity and welfare in the region. Liberal internationalism, with a pronounced social dimension, was generally the main ideological force in the collaboration of the Nordic countries.

The most significant manifestations of liberal internationalism in European politics in the postwar decades, however, were the establishment of the ECSC in 1952 and the EEC in 1957. It might be argued that the ECSC came about as an instrument of security rather than as a means to economic prosperity. Like the EDC, also planned in the early 1950s but eventually rejected by France, it was initially designed for the purpose of transforming Germany from a defeated enemy into a reliable ally and putting an end to the old rivalry between France and Germany. But as a protective measure it was different from the Western organizations set up in the late 1940s, which were designed to guard against an existing threat from outside the West, not against a potential danger from inside the circle of noncommunist powers. As a solution to the long-term problem for France and Europe of a powerful and assertive Germany, the ECSC was conceived in the liberal spirit of economic and legal-organizational internationalism. The idea of the Schuman Plan, from which it emerged, was to pool those resources that in the past had been essential for the conduct of war and to involve the potential rivals in the joint control of the coal and steel production of the region. While the pooling reflected the principle of efficient production through joint resources, the shared control expressed the idea of international organization through functional integration. Both practices could be seen as representing a development of traditional liberal internationalist tenets. If the merging of resources and markets was an extreme case of economic interdependence, the supranational control was an advanced form of institutional organization through transnational links. Both of them tended to transcend the pluralist order of the international system, and could be seen as harbingers of a federal structure for the region. But still the basic assumption behind the ECSC was that the political problems of international security and peace could be solved through economic harmony and international organization. And once the new institution had been firmly established, the joint efforts of its members were soon directed toward the liberal internationalist goal of economic prosperity.

While the ECSC dealt only with a particular sector of industry, the EEC followed the example of BENELUX and aimed for a full economic union. "It shall be the aim of the Community," the signatories of the Rome treaty stated in article 2, "by establishing a Common Market and progressively approximating the economic policies of Member States, to promote throughout the Community a harmonious development of economic activities, a continuous and balanced expansion, an increased stability, an accelerated raising of the standard of living and closer relations between its Member States." Reflecting the debate that had preceded the establishment of the Community, the treaty was a compromise between several approaches to European integration, but chiefly between the federal and the confederal way. In the first sentence of the preamble the signatories declared their determination "to establish the foundations of an ever closer union among the European peoples," but left it unclear what sort of union they had in mind. The clauses defining the nature and roles of the various bodies also betrayed a mixture of different constitutional ideas. While the Council of Ministers, made up of representatives of national governments, had the decision-making powers, the Commission, which enjoyed independence from the member states, had the sole right to submit proposals to the Council as well as the responsibility for implementing the decisions and ensuring that the members carried out their undertakings.

In the subsequent issue between federalists and confederalists, or supra-nationalists and intergovernmentalists, the former pinned their expectations on the Commission, which they hoped would develop into a federal government, and on the European Parliament, which they would like to be directly elected and be given new powers. Those who wanted a looser form of union, and were reluctant to go beyond institutionalized intergovernmental cooperation, insisted that the Council of Ministers should remain the dominant body. This debate was different from the issue between functionalists and neo-functionalists discussed earlier. That dispute, which was about different functional approaches to European integration, was largely between people of federal persuasions or inclinations. The debate between federalists and confederalists, about institutional goals and structural forms, had a broader focus and involved a wider range of people. It went through several phases, in which sometimes one side and sometimes the other had the upper hand.

The debate continued after 1967, when the EEC was merged with the ECSC and Euroatom to form the EC, and was still at the heart of the EU after the enlargement of membership in the following three decades. If European federalism in the years of the ECSC and EEC was conditioned by power-political considerations, mainly relating to the memory of WWII and the pressures of the cold war, in the period of the EC and EU it increasingly gained a momentum of its own. Reinforced by a strand of socialist internationalism, it became strong enough to maintain its position in the rivalry with confederalism and influential enough to provoke nationalist reactions of various kinds.

Although solidarist conservative internationalism, as shown in chapter 1, was an important influence particularly in the first several years of the EEC and although socialist internationalism of the democratic form, as will be shown in chapter 3, became a major influence at a later stage, the EEC/EC developed primarily as a manifestation of liberal internationalism. The Treaty of Rome, listing the future activities of the Community, started with the elimination of customs duties and quantitative restrictions on the import and export of goods between member states, the establishment of a common customs tariff and a common commercial policy toward third countries, and the abolition of the obstacles to the free movement of persons, services and capital between member states. Most of this program was a clear expression of the free-market philosophy at the root of economic liberal internationalism. But the application of the principles of that philosophy was limited to the area covered by the member states. The establishment of the common customs tariff and commercial policy toward third countries and, in particular, the inauguration of a common agricultural policy—politically the result of a deal between German industry and French agriculture that involved a fixing of prices and a consolidation of subsidies for agricultural products—turned out to be decidedly protectivist.

While the economic internationalism enshrined in the Common Market principles of the Rome treaty was geographically restricted, the legal-organizational form of internationalism intrinsic to the whole treaty was always more open. The projected closer union was never limited to the original signatories but was intended to be "among the European peoples." Britain, Denmark and Ireland joined the EC in 1973, Greece in 1981, Portugal and Spain in 1986 and Austria, Finland and Sweden in 1995, while other members were waiting to be admitted. Moreover, a growing number of overseas countries and territories enjoyed associate status. Thus, the EC turned out to be a closed common market of an ever-expanding group of states.

Above all, the EEC/EC was from the outset an organization for prosperity. Despite the pressures of the cold war and the fear of the Soviet Union and its allies, the aims of economic and social progress, as set out in the second sentence of the preamble of the Treaty of Rome, were goals in their own right rather than means to security. By the later 1950s, when NATO was taking care of military security and the economic organizations set up in the earlier years of the cold war were reducing the risk of subversion, the EEC was in a position to focus on economic progress through institutional integration. In subsequent decades, when social democratic internationalism became a growing influence in Community affairs, the focus of EC activities broadened. Public welfare through administrative control became an equally important part of the program. The coexistence of liberal and social democratic internationalism, manifested in some tension between liberal and socialist goals and policies, continued into the 1990s and seemed set to become a lasting feature of the ideology of the EU.

Among the less organized cases of institutionalized cooperation known as régimes, the most important manifestation of liberal internationalism in modern Europe has been that devoted to the protection of human rights. Set up during the cold war, this régime was initially limited to Western Europe but later, through a separate initiative, broadened to also cover other parts of Europe. The European Convention for the Protection of Human Rights and Fundamental Freedoms first met in 1950 and eventually produced the International Covenant on Civil and Political Rights. The Conference on Security and Cooperation in Europe met in Helsinki in 1973–5 and drew up the Helsinki Final Act. Initially little more than separate agreements about principles and rules, the régime gradually became institutionalized in the European Court of Human Rights as well as within domestic legal systems.[29] Defined largely in democratic terms, the rights and freedoms protected by the régime reflect mainly the individualistic values of liberal internationalism.

In Europe, as in many other parts of the world, liberal internationalism soon established itself as the dominant ideology after the cold war. The collapse of communist governments throughout Eastern Europe, the breakup of the Soviet Union and the dissolution of the Warsaw Treaty Organization made conventional security concerns much less pressing, and hence conservative internationalism less relevant. The demise of international communism and the triumph of Western capitalism made traditional socialist policies rather less promising, and thus socialist internationalism less appealing. The urgent need of most former communist countries for new political and economic systems, together with the marked preference of the United States and the major European powers for the establishment of democratic institutions and free markets in those countries, created favorable conditions for the ascendancy of liberal internationalism in most of Europe.

The invigorated internationalism that inspired the policies of most Western governments toward the former communist states, and sometimes also the policies of the governments of those countries themselves, went well beyond advancing the principles of liberal democracy and the doctrines of market economy. It also revived certain elements of liberal internationalism that had been important in earlier periods of European history but had become dormant during the cold war, preeminently the principle of national self-determination, the idea of humanitarian intervention and, to crown it all, faith in the UN as an instrument for underwriting international order. In the early 1990s, such internationalism found expression in a widespread optimism about the possibility of developing an international society of democratic nations and laying the foundations of a more orderly and just world.

However, the disturbing internal developments taking place in many of the former communist countries, the frustrations experienced by West European countries becoming diplomatically involved in the bloody conflicts within the former Yugoslavia, together with the possibility of their having to face similar, perhaps even greater, difficulties in relation to the former Soviet Union, shortly gave rise to a certain skepticism about the pursuit of liberal goals at large. The political events in some East European countries indicated just how difficult it could be to impose democratic systems on nations that had been under communist rule for more than forty years, and had had little or no prior tradition of democracy. The economic and social developments in such countries also revealed the dangers of suddenly freeing the markets of nations that for long had been under firm central control. The involvement of other countries in the crises and wars of the former Yugoslavia brought out the immense problems of applying the principle of national self-determination in regions where there were minorities within minorities, and the sheer impossibility of making that principle the sole basis of international order. It also demonstrated the difficulties of reconciling the traditional doctrine of national sovereignty with the recurrent practice of humanitarian intervention to defend minority rights and prevent or punish atrocities. Finally, the engagement of the UN in the attempt to restrain the warring parties in the former Yugoslavia and bring peace to the Balkans, showed once again how ineffectual a global international organization for peace and security could be. As a result of all those lessons, the initial optimism soon gave way to a greater realism in the pursuit of liberal policies.

The change of attitude was demonstrated most dramatically by the action over Kosovo in 1999. Abandoning the strictly diplomatic approach, which in dealings with the Serb leadership had proved futile, and ignoring the lack of a formal approval by the Security Council, which had been blocked by the Russian representative, the Western powers, acting through NATO, carried out a prolonged campaign of aerial bombardment of Serb strategic installations and armed forces in order to compel the nationalist government to stop its persecution of the Moslem population, withdraw its forces and accept an international occupation of the province. Though the means employed were drawn from the world of power politics, the ends pursued were essentially liberal, namely upholding the collective rights of an ethnic minority. Strongly backed by the American president and the British prime minister, the latter motivated by a new internationalism that was more liberal than socialist, the NATO campaign enjoyed the explicit or tacit support of most European governments and, with the exception of the Greeks, also the approval of large sections of the populations.

That liberal internationalism survived the disappointments of the early 1990s and remained the dominant ideology in European politics was not merely because the end of the cold war and the collapse of the Soviet Union had allowed competing forms of internationalism to recede, or because the growing strength of global economic, financial and technological forces facilitated the advance of an ideology that championed the notion of free markets. It was also for the reason that the values and goals of liberal internationalism were acceptable to most governments and people in Europe.

CHAPTER 3

Socialist Internationalism

T he third broad kind of internationalism that is manifested in modern European politics is part of socialist thought. Developed by European writers in the century after the Industrial Revolution, socialist thinking was already divided into two major branches in the late nineteenth century. One adhered to the doctrine of revolution as the means of social progress, while the other came to prefer a program of gradual reform of society. In the first half of the twentieth century the two branches moved further apart from each other and acquired separate identities. In the process, they developed different types of internationalism.

Origins and Development

The principal sources of the revolutionary tradition of socialist thought were the writings of Marx, Engels and Lenin. According to the interpretation of history developed by Marx and Engels, the revolutionary struggle of the proletariat would eventually overthrow the capitalist system of production and do away with the class structure of society, thus putting an end to exploitation and oppression of the workers. Since the state was the instrument of the ruling class, the abolition of the class system would lead to a withering of the state; and since war was violent conflict between states, the disappearance of states would mean the end of wars. Thus, the ultimate outcome of the historical process, according to their forecast and program, would be a world society distinguished by welfare, justice and peace.

For Marx and Engels, internationalism was the solidarity of the proletariat of the industrialized part of the world. They believed that class affinities were more binding than national allegiances, and that the bonds uniting the working classes of all countries would grow strong enough to enable the world proletariat to overthrow the existing structure of classes and states and replace it with a socialist world order. This faith in the transnational solidarity of the working classes was enshrined in the program and declarations of the Second International, which was founded by social democrats in 1889. In the period leading up to the outbreak of WWI, it became a theoretical basis for socialist strategy in crisis and war. According to a resolution drafted by this body in 1912, workers taking part in a war could only mean "shooting one another for the sake of the capitalists' profits, for the sake of the ambitions of dynasties, for the accomplishment of the aims of secret diplomatic treaties." Instead, socialists should see it as their duty to take advantage of the crisis by rousing the people against the capitalist order.[1]

That all the social democratic members of the German *Reichstag* only two years later, at the outbreak of WWI, voted for the war credits was a great disappointment for the more revolutionary socialists. Lenin saw it as an act of treason or desertion. But it was also a fact that revolutionary theorists had to take into account. Recognizing that support for the national war efforts, not only in Germany but also elsewhere in Europe, on that occasion had eclipsed the postulated solidarity of the working classes, Lenin reacted by stressing the importance of the revolutionary elite and spelling out the role of the leaders.

An even more formative influence on revolutionary socialist internationalism than the outbreak of WWI was the establishment of the Soviet Union. That the collapse of the Tsarist régime and the victory of the Bolsheviks, instead of sparking a general revolution in the capitalist world, led to civil war in Russia and intervention by capitalist states, and the fact that the Soviet Union survived these trials, created a situation that had not been foreseen by the socialist writers of the nineteenth century. Instead of the slow withering of states and eventual disappearance of national divisions, which were expected to do away with interstate relations and the need for foreign policies, came a gradual consolidation of the new state of the USSR and a long-term confrontation with the surrounding capitalist states. This called for some theorizing about relations between communist and noncommunist states. While Lenin helped lay the ideological foundations, Stalin and his ideologists formulated a theory that was based on the doctrine of socialism in one country.

The major lessons that Lenin drew were: that nations develop unevenly and do not all reach the revolutionary stage at the same time; that state divisions and national differences will survive for a very long time and will delay the eventual amalgamation of all nations; and that the existing proletarian state for the time being must be accepted as a necessary instrument for dealing with countries still in the capitalist stage of development. Stalin further postponed the disappearance of national differences and the withering of the state, focusing increasingly on the ideological implications of building a communist citadel in one country. The rise of fascism and the danger of war led him to insist that the state, in a situation of continued capitalist encirclement and renewed risk of military attack, had to remain strong and active. This development of the doctrine of socialism in one country, as we shall see, profoundly affected the socialist internationalism that became the ideological bond between the Soviet Union and the people's democracies after 1948. It also influenced the relationship between the Soviet leadership and the Communist parties in the noncommunist countries of Europe.

Although the emphasis in Soviet thinking between WWI and WWII shifted from the role of the international working class to the survival of the communist state, internationalism was still, at least most of the time, an important element in the communist strand of socialism. The ideological nature and political expression of such internationalism, however, underwent some changes. While Lenin, reacting to events, elaborated the concept of proletarian internationalism and modified the idea of world revolution, Trotsky insisted that the primary task should still be to foment revolution abroad. Stalin, though he reversed Trotsky's priorities and concentrated on developments within the Soviet Union, maintained the Communist International (COMINTERN), which had been set up in 1919. But he gradually turned it into an organ for supporting Soviet state interests rather than an instrument for instigating revolutions abroad, and finally dissolved the organization in 1943, after the Soviet Union had joined the allied powers in a coalition against the fascist powers. Yet, the bond between Moscow and the Communist parties in Europe, and elsewhere, survived the changing goals and priorities of the domestic and foreign policies of the Soviet Union. Motivated by the same political faith, inspired by the example of the Russian Revolution and impressed with the goals and achievements of the Soviet Union in peace and war, the Communist parties of the 1920s, 1930s, 1940s and much of the 1950s maintained discreet contact with Moscow and, on the whole, followed the ideological twists and turns of the Communist Party of the Soviet Union (CPSU).

The contrast in the interwar decades between two forms of internationalism, one serving the state interests of the Soviet Union and the other ministering to the transnational cause of socialists everywhere, can be seen as the source of much of the tension that after the middle of the century developed within the revolutionary strand of socialist internationalism. This tension led to disagreements between the Soviet leadership and the governments and parties of the people's democracies and to differences between Moscow and the Communist parties elsewhere in Europe.

The evolutionary tradition of socialist thought, which emerged on the Continent toward the end of the nineteenth century, started as a major revision of Marxist thought.[2] In both origin and development, it largely reflected the political experience of the German social democrats and some other European socialists in the later part of the century. Though based on the teachings of Marx and Engels, their policies soon became reformist in practice rather than revolutionary. Operating through the established political channels of each country, they pursued social improvement through progressive legislation. Once they had found that the machinery of state could be used for their own purposes, they worked to improve the state in each country rather than to undermine, overturn and destroy states everywhere. One of the first writers to draw theoretical conclusions from the social democratic experience was Edward Bernstein. His arguments, based mainly on the history of German social democrats and advanced in the last years of the century, amounted to a serious challenge to some central doctrines of Marxist theory.

The assertion that the proletariat has no fatherland, he observed, had not been borne out by experience. Despite their transnational links, the socialists in each country had, in fact, pursued the interests of the national proletariat and had worked largely within the conventional confines of their state. Further, the socialists did not seem to have been inspired by the ultimate goal of the withering of the state proclaimed by earlier Marxists. Focusing instead on more immediate goals, they had sought to turn the state into an instrument for the pursuit of the social, economic and political aims of socialism. Marxist doctrines about the proletariat and the state, Bernstein concluded, were in need of revision.

Together with the revisionists of the early twentieth century, he replaced the old ideal of a peaceful world society, reached through proletarian revolution, destruction of the class system and withering of the states, with the goal of an international society of reformed states, all cooperating in the solution of common problems. Like the liberal tradition of internationalism, this form of socialist internationalism rested on the assumption that governments representing the people would be more rational and moral than governments of nondemocratic states and that their relations with each other would be more harmonious and peaceful. Like liberal reform of the political system and free trade among nations, socialist reform of society and transnational relations among peoples would do away with the old international politics of alliances, power balances and recurrent wars. Like liberal internationalism, this kind of socialist internationalism rested ultimately on the assumption that international politics could be pacified only through a reform of domestic politics. Thus for both liberals and socialists, domestic politics preceded international politics. But the two internationalist traditions differed on the kind of domestic reform to be pursued and on the nature of transnational relations to be developed. While the objective of liberal internationalism was the prosperity of nations, the concern of socialist internationalism was more with the equality and welfare of people.

The experience of WWI, when the German social democrats voted for the war credits and when working men in all belligerent nations joined the armed forces of their countries and fought for the war aims of their governments, strengthened the revisionist case against the notion of a transnational solidarity of the world proletariat. So did the advance of various European Social Democratic and Labor parties and movements in the interwar years. The stronger they became and the closer they moved to governmental office, the more determined their leaders were to use the state as an instrument for realizing their political program. The tendency, already apparent in prewar Europe, to shift attention away from distant goals for world politics and to concentrate efforts on the immediate programs for domestic affairs, became more pronounced. But, despite the national introversion, the revisionist brand of socialist internationalism survived. It took the form partly of a development of established modes of transnational relations among parties and movements and partly of a new and growing interest in international organization at governmental levels. In the heyday of the League of Nations, socialist internationalism followed liberal internationalism in pursuing institutionalization of international relations. After the breakdown of the League of Nations and the coming of WWII, however, social democrats and other revisionist socialists once again rallied behind their governments.

After 1945 the revolutionary and the reformist tradition of socialist thought continued their separate courses, each presenting its own varieties of internationalism. The revolutionary, or communist, tradition comprised two major strands of internationalism, one extending to transnational relations of communist parties and movements in noncommunist countries and one confined to relations among states already set on the path toward socialism. Both were directed from Moscow, and marked by a tendency to put Soviet interests first both in the formulation of theory and in the application of principles. The strand of internationalism aimed at communist parties and sympathizers in capitalist countries provoked criticism and opposition from Trotskyites, Maoists, anarchists and others who rejected the teachings of

Stalin and his successors and looked elsewhere for ideological guidance. Within the West European communist parties themselves, there was growing disagreement with Soviet ideas and policies. In the 1970s, large sections of some major parties rebelled against Soviet tutelage and asserted their independence, eventually becoming known as Eurocommunists.

The strand of internationalism covering relations between the Soviet Union and the communist countries of Eastern Europe also produced negative reactions from some of the parties involved. The record of Marshal Tito, who had already asserted his independence of Moscow at the time when the people's democracies had first accepted Soviet control of their internal affairs and external relations, was an occasional source of inspiration for dissatisfied leaders. The collapse of communist governments throughout Europe in the late 1980s and early 1990s put an end to both strands of communist internationalism in European politics.

The reformist, whether laborite or social democratic, tradition of socialist thought also presented, at least in principle, two strands of internationalism, namely an older one referring to transnational relations among working-class parties, trade unions and other movements and a more modern one relating to involvement in the activities of intergovernmental organizations or European institutions. But the former was usually rather less substantial than its revolutionary counterpart. Either it was largely eclipsed by unflinching engagement in the national pursuit of socialist goals or it was to some extent subsumed in a less or more wholehearted commitment to pursuit of the same goals through the institutional channels of international organizations. Thus, in the first postwar decades most of the European Labor and Social Democratic parties concentrated their political activities on the national stage, on the assumption that the more promising way of achieving social progress in Europe was through parallel national efforts rather than through international cooperation. At the same time, however, they tried to keep up the old tradition of cultivating transnational bonds at nongovernmental levels. In the following decades, both the political parties and the trade unions became more Europeanist. Recognizing that socialist programs might be introduced and developed more easily and effectively through some of the institutions that were emerging in Western Europe, many of their leaders became inspired by a revived internationalism, which focused on institutionalized cooperation among governments and parties with progressive views.

The present description and discussion of the revolutionary and reformist types of socialist internationalism will concentrate, on the one hand, on the internationalism that tied the people's democracies to the Soviet Union and, on the other hand, on the internationalism that inspired the reformist efforts of labor and social democratic governments and parties within the new institutions of Western Europe.

Revolutionary Socialist Internationalism

The form of internationalism that in the age of high tension and intermittent détente in East–West relations became the unifying ideology of Eastern Europe, began to take shape only after 1948. In that year the people's democracies, as they soon became known, emerged as states with an identifiable character. Still under the control of the Red Army, which three or four years earlier had liberated them from German occupation and Nazi rule, they installed governments of the Stalinist type foisted upon them by Moscow and established political and economic structures modeled on those of the Soviet Union. With the emergence of such a group of states, adjacent to each other and all set on the path toward socialism, arose the need for a theory to guide relations among communist countries. Thus, a new theory, developed in the last years of Stalin's rule and revised in the following decades by Soviet ideologists and leading theorists of the East European régimes, took its place alongside two rather more elaborate Soviet theories of international relations, namely that pertaining to relations with the old states of the capitalist West and that applying to relations with the new countries of the Third World.

As already pointed out, the East European internationalism had important elements in common with conservative internationalism. First, it was, though not solely, a theory about interstate relations; second, it was, as it turned out, largely a guide to intergovernmental cooperation, not least for the purposes of security and defense; and third, it was, as an ideological basis for international organization, distinctly of the hegemonic kind, reflecting the power and authority of the Soviet Union within the region. But in both origins and essence it was a socialist theory. Derived from proletarian internationalism, it was about relations between classes and political parties, namely the communist parties of the Soviet Union and the people's democracies. Designed to meet the needs of the members of the socialist commonwealth and adapted to the relative uniformity of their political, economic and social structures, it was ultimately aimed at socialist goals. In its socialist aspect, this theory underwent several changes between the last years of Stalin's rule and the arrival of Gorbachev. They were closely linked with developments in the political relationship between the Soviet Union and the people's democracies.

The imposition of Stalinist régimes in Eastern Europe, the expulsion of Tito's Yugoslavia from the emerging bloc and the establishment of the

Communist Information Agency (COMINFORM) and other regional organizations were accompanied by the expansion of the doctrine of socialism in one country into an axiom of socialism in one bloc. But the broadening of the concept did not lead to a move toward equality among the members of the bloc. The new régimes of Eastern Europe, which were presented as a form of dictatorship of the proletariat exercised through the leadership of the communist parties, were ideologically as dependent on the authority of Moscow as they were politically on the power of the Soviet Union. As long as Stalin lived, Soviet domination of the bloc continued unabated.

After the death of Stalin, and especially after Khrushchev's denunciation of his rule at the 20th party congress in 1956, national reactions to the policy and practice of always giving priority to Soviet interests occurred in one people's democracy after another. Khrushchev, apparently hoping to move away from the Stalinist type of coercion toward a more voluntary solidarity, for which he reintroduced the term proletarian internationalism, reacted to the new pressures by stressing the special quality of relations among socialist countries and holding out the prospect of greater equality. On this basis he set out to woo Tito's Yugoslavia back into the bloc. When the attempt failed, and persistent tendencies toward various national forms of communism, in Soviet terminology described as revisionism, continued to threaten the leading role of the Soviet Union and endanger the cohesion of the bloc, a new stress on recognition of Soviet leadership and acceptance of the need for unity entered the ideological debate. At the same time, however, there was still some acknowledgment of the importance of national interests and special needs. Proletarian internationalism and socialist patriotism, party ideologies asserted, went hand in hand in fraternal friendship. Such internationalism, which provided the ideological support for interparty relations, and respect for the equality and independence of members of the bloc, which laid the legal and political foundations for interstate relations, were the ingredients of the ideological structure now called socialist internationalism.

Many of the recurring discussions about the expediency of moving from a rather narrow focus on Soviet needs and concerns toward a broader consideration of the interests of all members of the bloc, which characterized the debate in the late 1950s, had to do with matters of international economics. Stalin's successors tried to strengthen the cohesion of the bloc by coordinating the economic plans of the members and imposing a division of labor upon them. But they came up against difficulties. As in the political field, conflict of interests led to substantial issues with some of the other states. Representatives of several people's democracies defended their economic interests with a determination that was sometimes reinforced by popular nationalist feelings.[3] Soviet ideologists liked to present such issues in terms of national interests of states and shared interests of the socialist commonwealth, by which they usually meant bloc unity under Soviet leadership. They insisted that the particular and the general interests were in harmony with each other, given that all parties pursued correct policies, and maintained that conflict between them was bound to be nonantagonistic, temporary and untypical, and hence easy to deal with.[4] Other theorists, especially Yugoslav officials and writers, whose views were reflected in some East European statements and writings of the time, saw no such natural harmony. They asserted the right to mutual respect between communist countries and defended the principle of noninterference in the affairs of others.

With both the political and the economic issues unresolved, the ideological debate continued in the 1960s and subsequent decades. It was conditioned by recurrent or continuous tension between states or parties in three regions of the communist world, namely between members of the bloc, between the bloc and Yugoslavia and between the Soviet Union and China. In each region the discord between the parties produced reiterations, clarifications or reinterpretations of the communist theory of socialist internationalism. Intra-bloc differences were usually presented in terms of disagreement about alternative paths to socialism. In extreme cases they would lead to open conflict, in the form of armed intervention under Soviet leadership and toppling of a recalcitrant government, as in Prague in 1968. This event was followed by a reiteration of the doctrine of fraternal mutual aid, which after the invasion of Budapest in 1956, had already been described as an integral part of relations among socialist countries and an effective expression of the principle of socialist internationalism.[5] An article published in *Pravda* a month after the invasion of Czechoslovakia proclaimed that it was not only the right but also the duty of socialist states to come to the defense of socialism whenever it was threatened.[6]

Relations between the bloc and Yugoslavia continued to provide occasions for redefining and clarifying the orthodox theory of socialist internationalism. Tito's emphasis on the principles of mutual respect and noninterference among all socialist countries was seen as opening the way for divisive forms of national communism, which might challenge the political and ideological leadership of the Soviet Union and undermine the unity of the bloc. To guard against such dangers, orthodox ideologists in the Soviet Union and elsewhere denounced revisionism and warned against the temptations of nationalism, still affirming the harmony of national and bloc interests.

In the early 1960s the Chinese challenge to Soviet hegemony in the communist world also led to ideological introspection within the bloc and various clarifications of the doctrines of socialist internationalism. An early attempt, made in 1960, to reach a compromise between Soviet and Chinese views took the form of a warning against excessive emphasis on national peculiarities and a call for a proper combination of socialist internationalism and socialist patriotism.[7] The attempt failed, and soon the Sino-Soviet differences broke out in open ideological confrontation. In an increasingly hostile exchange of words, which usually turned on the correct interpretation of passages in the writings of the socialist fathers, Maoist China was accused of the heresy of "dogmatism." The Chinese responded by accusing the Russians of "revisionism." When the Albanian régime broke with Moscow and lined up with Peking, the Chinese found their first ideological allies within the bloc. Thus, the Soviet version of socialist internationalism was developed and defined in opposition to the double heresy of revisionism and dogmatism. While each divergence from orthodoxy was championed by the government of a country outside the bloc, it was also reflected in the statements and policies of one or more régimes within the bloc.

The entire ideological debate was more about means than ends. Indeed, focusing on disagreement about the correct path to socialism tended to obscure a broad though vague consensus about goals. The existence of such a consensus allowed proponents of socialist internationalism to base their appeals on the need for unity in the defense of socialist achievements and the struggle with capitalism and imperialism. The socialist goals and achievements were mentioned in bilateral treaties of friendship and documents of various international organizations of the bloc. Some were also spelled out in the constitution of the Soviet Union and the founding documents of other communist régimes as well as in the programs and statements of communist parties, both the ruling ones in the East and those in Western Europe. They were of an economic and social nature and related to the welfare of the people. Freedom from exploitation, of the kind endured by the workers under the capitalist system, was high on the list. From this flowed a number of rights, some of which were set out in the Soviet constitution, such as the right to work, leisure, health care, pensions, housing, education and to sharing cultural achievements.[8] The emphasis was on the equality of the masses in the enjoyment of the material goods of society.

The history of relations between Moscow and the West European communist parties since the late 1940s showed much the same conflict between the interests of the Soviet Union and the CPSU and those of the other communist parties, and much the same tension between the doctrine of

Soviet control and the principle of independence as characterized the inter-action of the Soviet Union and the people's democracies. Again the concept of socialist internationalism was at the heart of the ideological issue. Here, too, the debate revolved around the opposition between the precept of unity, as conceived by Moscow, and the principle of diversity, as fitfully advanced by other communist parties. At the height of the cold war the stress was very much on unity. Despite the historical and cultural differences between Soviet and West European communism, the Western parties accepted political lead-ership and ideological control from Moscow till well after the end of Stalin's rule. After Khrushchev's denunciation of Stalin, however, the emphasis in interparty debate began to shift toward national diversity. In prolonged efforts to maintain unity and control, the Soviet Union organized several international party conferences in the late 1950s and the 1960s, which passed a number of formal resolutions. But the principles of equality and independence of all parties were underlined, and criticism of Soviet direction of the communist movement was voiced.

In the course of the 1960s the estrangement between Moscow and several West European parties intensified. Rejecting Soviet attempts to revitalize the concept of proletarian internationalism, one party after another began to entertain new ideas about internationalism, which were based mainly on recognition of the autonomy and equality of each party.[9] In each case, the process of disengagement from Moscow tutelage was accompanied by much debate within the party, which in some instances led to splits and the for-mation of new parties. By the mid-1970s the new, more independent orientation of most communist parties was so marked that the term Eurocommunism gained currency as a description of the diverse manifesta-tions of liberal and national tendencies.[10]

Although some of the reformed communist parties suffered electoral setbacks in the late 1970s, the emergence of Eurocommunism meant a soft-ening of some political and ideological divisions in Europe. In East–West relations it helped to weaken the polarization of the cold war. In the politi-cal life of individual West European countries it signified a degree of con-vergence between the ideas and policies of the communist parties and the noncommunist socialist parties. To some extent inspired by the nationalist tendencies that in the 1960s and 1970s affected other parties as well, the Eurocommunists, too, became more inclined to think in national rather than international terms. Like the socialist left, they were prepared to eschew vio-lent means and to pursue their goals in more peaceful ways, such as through parliamentary alliances or ad hoc cooperation with other political parties. Though in the last resort perhaps not all of them were willing to accept the limitations of the democratic process of parliamentary politics, in their increasingly reformist approach to the transformation of society they came much closer to the social democratic left.

Reformist Socialist Internationalism

In the late 1940s and most of the 1950s the majority of the political parties that advocated socialism through reform, whether they called themselves socialists, social democrats or labor, concentrated their efforts on the national political scene. Though some of them, notably those of the three BENELUX countries, were already Europeanist at that early stage, most were against the drive to unite Europe, or Western Europe, which was then gathering momentum. Like most of the nonsocialist leftist parties of those years, they could not embrace an economic, political and cultural movement that was associated with capitalist, Catholic and reactionary forces and dedicated to the creation of some form of union in which the newly reconstituted West Germany would have a primary role. Also they could not be enthusiastic about the possibility of being able to pursue their goals through the projected European institutions, which might stand in the way of their traditional efforts within the existing, and hence more solid and reliable, national political institutions. To switch from the national to the European level of activity, they considered, might well mean a postponement of socialist planning and organization.

Within their countries, the democratic socialist parties pursued the goals of equality, justice and welfare through economic and social reform. In the course of laying the foundations of the modern welfare state, many parties became more absorbed in the practicalities of improving the economic and social conditions of the people in the immediate situation than in the long-term project of doing away with capitalism and preparing the way for socialism. While some parties, notably the Labor Party governing Britain in the early postwar years, nationalized key industries, others began to lose interest in the old question of the ownership of the means of production and to accept the welfare state as the ultimate goal of reform.

Formal transnational relations among the political parties and movements during this period of self-absorption were mainly at local levels, for example, between the Nordic social democrats, and usually not of a particularly substantial nature. At the European level there was remarkably little cooperation, considering the solid numerical strength of social democrats and other West European democratic socialists. Yet, the internationalist spirit had not died completely. There was still an assumption that the reformist socialist program of rational control of the political process, judicious planning for economic growth and earnest pursuit of public welfare could also have a beneficial effect on the international conduct of the state. A government that pressed for a more egalitarian society and cared about the welfare of the people, it was thought, was more likely to be pacific in its foreign policy than governments with other concerns. The advent of pacific governments in a number of countries, it was concluded, would change the climate of international relations, reduce the element of conflict, facilitate friendly cooperation and thus make peace more secure. It was an internationalism that rested on parallel but largely separate economic planning and social reform. As in liberal internationalism, particularly its radical version, according to which, too, international harmony and peace would follow national reform and improvement, the underlying doctrine was still, as it had been since the revisionists at the turn of the century, the primacy of domestic politics. But the reformist socialists of the postwar period, like their predecessors earlier in the century, were more engrossed with their domestic program than most liberal internationalists.

The socialists of the following decades, too, gave priority to the goals of justice and welfare for the people. The difference was that they gradually discovered that some of the institutions and machinery of the new European Communities could be useful in the pursuit of their political, economic and social aims. This eventually led most of them to subscribe to a Europeanized form of socialist internationalism. While the Dutch and Belgian socialists had become Europeanized at an early stage, the socialist parties in the other original EEC countries had either been divided on the issue, as in the French and Italian cases, or been against a European union, as in the case of the German party, which had been more interested in German unification. The change in the attitude of these parties came in the late 1950s and early 1960s. For the parties of the six countries that joined the Community at later stages the change took longer. Neither the British Labor Party nor the Danish Social Democrats were able to accept the federalist tendencies. When the socialist parties of Greece, Spain and Portugal eventually expressed some support for European policies, it was generally more for reasons to do with their national problems and policies than because of real enthusiasm for a united Europe.

Despite the late conversion of some and the lack of conviction of others, the socialist parties shortly became the most integrationist group in the EC. As in domestic politics, they believed in a big government and worked for democratic control, economic planning and social reform. Their efforts in the early 1960s marked a revival of interest in the federalist approach.

The European federalism of the first postwar years had come mainly from those noncommunist leftist sections of the antifascist resistance movements that had promoted the idea of a United States of Europe as a way of overcoming nationalism and putting an end to war on the continent. Though it had enjoyed wide currency in the first years after 1945, especially in countries that had been occupied by Germany, this federalism had failed to produce any substantial political results and had gone into decline after the onset of the cold war. In the early 1950s a different strand of federalism had found expression in the abortive projects for European Political and Defense Communities. Federalism had also been one of several ideological influences that had left their mark on the founding treaties of the EEC. In the first period of both the ECSC and the EEC, however, the integrationist efforts had on the whole followed the functional approach of Eurocrats convinced of the virtues of working through economic, social and technical sectors rather than the direct political way of those preferring to set up a supranational entity by constitutional methods. Now the Europeanization of most of the socialist parties represented in the EC led to a shift of emphasis in the approach to integration. In the following decades the federal idea became the main impulse in the development of the EC.

The socialist support for the EC program of economic and political union had several qualities that distinguished it from the policies of some other supporters of the program. First, the socialists insisted that the institutions and work of the EC should rest on the principle of popular legitimacy. To that end, they called for enhanced powers for the European Parliament and direct elections of its members. Instead of a Europe of states or fatherlands, as the intergovernmentalists and confederalists had projected, or a Europe of bureaucrats or offices, as the patrician Eurocrats and early functionalists had created, they worked for a Europe of the peoples, as they put it.

Second, they had a special interest in the social dimension of the projected union, which reflected their long-established concern with public welfare. For most of them, the social chapter of the Maastricht treaty became a key plank in their program. That some socialists, for example, the Danish Socialist People's Party and SDP, were either opposed to or ambiguous in their support for this part of the treaty largely because the social measures stipulated, in their opinion, did not go far enough, only underlined the importance most European socialists attached to a system of social reform under administrative control. In addition to such traditional preoccupations, the socialists of that period paid much more attention than before to ecological considerations, especially after the emergence of the parties of the Greens that challenged the existing socialist parties from the left.

Third, the socialists had a more bureaucratic approach to European integration than most other parties. Both their long-standing preoccupations with social justice and material welfare and their novel interests in environmental safeguards called for a highly developed central administration with machinery for effective control. Thus, the Europeanist socialists became the party group of big government in the new Europe.

Since their integrationist efforts through official channels usually went hand in hand with more unofficial contacts between their parties, the organizational internationalism of the Europeanized socialists had both a supranational and a transnational dimension. Within the EC, however, the latter tended to be subsumed under the former. But socialist internationalism in noncommunist Europe was never confined to the fields of activity defined by the Communities. It was extended to other noncommunist parts of Europe as well as to the world beyond, in both spheres of which it presented a marked transnational aspect. This came out most clearly in the ideas and activities of some leading social democratic internationalists of the period.

The foremost example was Willy Brandt, governing mayor of Berlin during part of the cold war, later foreign minister and eventually chancellor of the Federal Republic. His political life went far beyond involvement in German and EC affairs and had both a wider European and a global dimension. In EC politics he set his hopes high and never deviated from the central idea of union. Speculating about the future at the end of the 1980s, he thought that the Community was on the brink of a qualitative leap forward. After the introduction of the single market, he predicted, the monetary union would begin to take shape and a harmonization of the laws of taxation and social welfare would come about. Would the EU, by which he meant something going far beyond the coordination of foreign policy, crown such a development, he wondered?[11] Despite various promising institutional developments, however, he still had some concerns. One was to do with the democratic anchorage and control of the Community, which remained underdeveloped and unsatisfactory.[12] Already when he had taken his seat in the European Parliament in 1979, after the first direct elections, his aim had been first to enlarge the competence of the institution and then to determine its constitution through national elections.[13] His other concern related to the achievements of the EC in the field of social welfare, which he still found quite inadequate. At the Paris summit meeting in October 1972 he had tabled a memorandum on European social union. Social progress, he had argued, was not to be seen as a mere appendage of economic growth. "If we develop a European perspective on social policy, many of the citizens of our states will find it easier to identify with the Community."[14]

It was in his involvement with European politics beyond the EC and with world affairs that Brandt's transnational internationalism was most apparent. One of the European issues in which he had taken some interest was the fate of social democracy in Southern Europe. Unfortunately, it had not been possible for him to establish close links with Andreas Papandreou, who had shown little interest in coming to terms with European social democracy. But he was proud that the SPD, under his leadership, had done something to help Spanish democracy to its feet, and that he personally had intervened to support Felipe Gonzales. He also recalled how in 1975, at a conference in Stockholm of friendly heads of governments and party leaders, he had suggested setting up a committee to defend democracy in Portugal against the threat of a communist *putsch*.[15] In transnational relations he apparently attached much importance to contact between party leaders. His relations with Bruno Kreisky in Austria and Olof Palme in Sweden were particularly close. Meeting from time to time to discuss world events, the three leaders also published a little book of their conversations and letters to each other. "All three of us," Brandt pointed out, "led large and influential parties, and we were friends who could discuss anything, and had power to make things happen."[16]

For a long time he had liked to establish contact and maintain relations with similar political parties and groups in other parts of the world, so he accepted the presidency of the Socialist International in 1976. First founded in Paris in 1889 under the name of the Second International, it had been revived in Frankfurt in 1951 as a loose association of social democratic parties but had led a rather shadowy existence. Setting out to reinvigorate it, Brandt helped it to overcome its traditional Eurocentrism. Its main areas of interest became East–West as well as North–South relations, together with human rights and the environment. Regionally it concentrated its efforts on Central America, South Africa and the Middle East. Reviewing his experience of this "Social Democratic working community of independent national parties," he found that all it could do was to exchange notes and compare experiences, summarize opinions and influence international and national decision-making, but that this could be of considerable importance in helping to limit conflict and bringing new ideas to the forefront. The experience of cooperation at party level had also reinforced his confidence in the regional approach to the handling of international questions.[17] Brandt's commitment to global and regional transnationalism reflected a belief in an ever-growing list of interests shared by all states and in the emergence of a more developed world society of independent nations.

Relieved of his governmental duties in 1974, Brandt was able to devote more attention to global issues, such as the growth of the earth's population, the exhaustion of its natural resources and the damage to the environment. But his new outlook was not merely a result of a change in his personal fortunes. It also reflected more general tendencies toward a deepening as well as a widening of the transnationalism of social democrats and other reformist socialists in the late 1970s and the 1980s. Thus, while the revolutionary strand, in the form of the communist internationalism of Eastern Europe, became more state-centered over the years, the reformist strand of socialist internationalism in Western Europe moved in the opposite direction and became rather more transnational. In the aggregate, however, socialist internationalism in all parts of Europe since WWII showed a broad tendency fairly similar to that of conservative internationalism in the same period. While the more solidarist versions, as championed by Moscow, were more in evidence in the earlier postwar decades, the more pluralist versions, as presented by reformist socialists, gained ascendancy in the later decades. The shift from the former to the latter was completed with the decline of communist internationalism in the late 1980s and its virtual disappearance as a political force in the early 1990s.

Influence and Manifestations

The communist version of socialist internationalism, how ever it was defined by the régimes concerned, conditioned relations among parties and governments in Eastern Europe and influenced both the form of treaties and the style of cooperation between the Soviet Union and the people's democracies. Bilateral treaties of friendship and cooperation, ostensibly concluded in the spirit of socialist internationalism, were usually said to be aimed at strengthening the internationalist bonds between the contracting parties. The major multilateral organizations were also, in some way or other, manifestations of such internationalism. Both the CMEA and the WTO, despite the already noted similarities with their counterparts in Western Europe, were expressions of socialist internationalism not merely by definition.[18] In a more real sense, they were products of that belief system.

In spite of occasional attempts by the Soviet Union to introduce supranational elements in economic planning, the CMEA remained, as we have seen, largely an agency for intergovernmental cooperation. Moreover, since its ultimate purpose turned out to be the laying of the economic foundations for an integrated defense of the Soviet-led bloc, it had a good deal in common with those West European organizations that, because of their link with security concerns, have been treated here as essentially manifestations of conservative internationalism. But, in its origins, nature, activities and goals, the CMEA was still a socialist organization. Set up by the communist governments of the Soviet Union and the people's democracies, it reflected the shared identity of the countries of the socialist commonwealth. In the pursuit of economic growth through coordination, it prepared an international socialist division of labor that was intended to be quite different from the capitalist division of labor. Aimed at a continued rise in the productivity of the countries and a steady increase in the well being of the peoples, its overall aim was to strengthen socialism.

The WTO, though essentially an agency for intergovernmental cooperation for security purposes, was also in several respects a manifestation of socialist internationalism. Like the CMEA, it reflected the shared identity of its members. It reflected the relations characteristic of a socialist commonwealth, which were thought to be different, and of a higher nature, than relations among capitalist countries. Designed to coordinate the military forces of the members of the bloc, it was an organization for the defense of socialist achievements against imperialist enemies. Even in intra-bloc affairs, it could be a guardian of these achievements. This was the rationale for presenting the Brezhnev doctrine as a principle of socialist internationalism according to which the collective interests of the socialist commonwealth took precedence over the national inclinations of member states. The collapse of the people's democracies and breakup of the Soviet Union and subsequent experiments with democratic government and market economy soon put an end to the various organizational manifestations of the communist version of socialist internationalism.

The broad democratic strand of socialist internationalism in the noncommunist parts of Europe found expression in a considerable variety of institutions, some in the form of interparty fora and others of intergovernmental organizations. One of the former, namely Socialist International, eventually became quasi-global both in its membership and in its fields of interest. Others were local, and more or less informal. An example was SCANDILUX, a forum set up in 1980 by social democrats and socialists from Scandinavia and the BENELUX countries for the discussion of security, arms control and related matters. Exchanging information and discussing policy alternatives, the representatives, who included French, British and German observers, had some influence on the policies of the parties. At the regional level, the Confederation of the Socialist Parties of the European Community, established in 1974, helped to coordinate policies in many fields.

The majority of the institutions evincing socialist internationalist influence, however, were intergovernmental organizations founded by multilateral treaties. Most of them were devoted to specific fields of economic and social activity, for example, transport, communications, science, culture, health or ecology, and were in the nature of standing agencies set up to serve governments prepared to cooperate in the particular area. To the extent that such organizations were devoted ultimately to the pursuit of welfare, each within its own section, they could be seen as, at least partly, manifestations of the influence of socialist internationalism.

Rather more important were those intergovernmental organizations that were set up with a much broader charge and were directed toward some form of integration. The best example at the local level may be the institutional framework for Nordic cooperation. The Nordic Council, established by Denmark, Iceland, Norway and Sweden in 1952 and joined by Finland three years later, included all the Nordic countries and three autonomous territories, namely Greenland, the Faeroes and Åland. Consisting of members of the parliaments and representatives of the governments and with a presidium to supervise its work between sessions, it was conceived as an organ for initiating, following up and encouraging Nordic cooperation. The Council of Ministers, set up in 1971, became the implementing organ. The names of the standing committees—the Economic, the Legal, the Communications, the Cultural, the Social and Environmental, and the Budget and Control— indicated the main areas of cooperation. In contrast with the European Communities, which started their efforts at cooperation and integration mainly with goods and capital and only much later turned to people, the Nordic institutions started with the needs of individuals and only later put other kinds of issues on the agenda as well. The principal achievements were a common labor market, a nearly common social security system, a high degree of juridical coordination, long-standing cultural cooperation, effective coordination of transport and communications, substantial ecological, economic and financial cooperation as well as a free market. The latter however was achieved mainly through the European Free Trade Area (EFTA) and EC. While issues of European policy in particular and foreign policy in general were discussed habitually in later years, no common foreign or security policy was reached. The major efforts and achievements were in the fields of social, cultural, economic and ecological relations, and reflected more than any other influences the social democratic concerns with welfare.

At the regional level, the most important expression of the democratic form of socialist internationalism was through the treaties and activities of the EC. Already the treaty of Rome had "an accelerated raising of the standard of living" among its aims. Though the focus was very much on the establishment of a common market, the list of intended activities of the new

Community included "the creation of a European Social Fund in order to improve the possibilities of employment for workers and to contribute to the raising of their standard of living."[19] But it was not till the following decades, when the Social Democrats and the Radical Liberal parties began to recognize that the EC could be made to serve their economic and social goals, that socialist internationalism became a substantial ideological input in Community politics and activities, strong enough to rival the well-established liberal internationalist influence.

The foremost manifestations of socialist internationalism in EC affairs in more recent years were the Social Charter of 1989 and the social chapter of the treaty on EU, better known as the Maastricht treaty, negotiated and signed the following years. The signatories of the latter document, except the United Kingdom, composed a protocol on social policy, in which they agreed to continue along the path indicated in the Social Charter, and followed up with an agreement on aims and procedures. Article I of this agreement stated that "the Community of the Member States shall have as their objectives the promotion of employment, improved living and working conditions, proper social protection, dialogue between management and labor, the development of human resources with a view to lasting high employment and the combatting of exclusion . . . ." One of the principles laid down was that of equal treatment of men and women in the labor market. The final article required the Commission to prepare an annual report on progress in achieving the stated objectives and forward it to the European Parliament, the Council and the Economic and Social Committee. It also empowered the European Parliament to invite the Commission to draw up reports on particular social problems. The broad concerns behind these documents were clearly with welfare and social justice.

Other ways in which socialist internationalism expressed itself within the EC were through support for the drive for democratization of the institution and backing for the call for deeper integration of the Community. Having recognized the usefulness of the EC for their purposes, the social democrats soon came to see a need for much tighter public control of the complex organization. As mentioned, they called for increased powers for the European Parliament and direct election of its members. Accepting that the EC could be much more than an instrument of capitalist interests, they and their political allies pushed for more advanced integration of the Community, some of their efforts indicating a preference for the sort of tight administrative web often associated with the concept of neo-functionalism. Soon the socialist demand for "big government" came into conflict with the liberal preference for minimal intervention. Thus the EC, and subsequently the EU, became a battleground for the two rivaling forms of internationalism.

Around the middle of the twentieth century, solidarist internationalisms of various kinds were quite prominent in European political thought. While leftist federalism gained currency in many countries in the first years after 1945, rightist federalism became prevalent in some Catholic countries in the first postwar decade. During the same period, the Stalinist version of socialist internationalism reigned in Eastern Europe. After the start of the cold war, however, solidarist approaches to European integration were soon eclipsed by pluralist efforts at intergovernmental cooperation. In the West, pluralist conservative internationalism soon prevailed over all other sorts of internationalism. In the East, potentially pluralist principles and practices of military, political and economic cooperation among communist states gradually qualified the solidarist doctrines and policies of Stalinist socialist internationalism.

The second postwar decade saw liberal internationalism reassert itself in the international organization of Western Europe, particularly through the EEC. Subsequently socialist internationalism, too, established itself in West European politics, at both local and regional levels. Thus, after the late 1940s the overall ideological development was a progression from conservative toward liberal and socialist internationalism. While conservative internationalism remained a major influence in the international organization of the region, the central tension in the EC was between liberal and socialist internationalism.

The shift from the conservative toward the two other kinds of internationalism meant a change of focus from states and interstate relations toward nations and peoples and transnational relations, and from intergovernmental cooperation toward integration and union. It also involved a turn from high politics toward international economics and European society, and from security toward prosperity and welfare. The latter development reflected not only an overriding desire for material progress and social justice but also a conviction that the ultimate causes of conflict and war were economic and social, and a belief that peace and security could be achieved through economic progress and social improvement. The broad shift from conservatism toward liberalism and socialism in West European internationalism was conditioned by, first, an enduring stability and then waves of détente in East–West relations, and eventually by the petering out of the cold war. In the early 1990s it became possible, and sometimes necessary, for most of Western and much of Eastern Europe to concentrate attention on the economic and social scene.

Strictly speaking, the various kinds of internationalism examined here all appeared in a regionalist shape, in the sense that their geographical scope was Europe or, more often, some part of Europe. Conceptually, however, most of them transcended that part of the world. The conservative internationalism of intergovernmental cooperation for security purposes, as represented in NATO, comprehended the whole area covered by the alliance and had its strategic center of gravity in North America. The liberal internationalism of free trade and economic prosperity, as expressed primarily in GATT and the World Trade Organization, in principle comprised most of the world. Socialist internationalism, in both its communist and its social democratic version, had also a quasi-global dimension, discernible in diplomatic relations or transnational links. Moreover, internationalisms of various kinds appeared in other continents, and found expression in regional organizations such as the Organization of American States (1948), the Organization of African Unity (1963) and the Association of South East Asian Nations (1967). Yet, internationalism in the second half of the twentieth century was so concentrated in Europe that it became primarily a European phenomenon. Conditioned by the structure of the global system and the state of European politics, it was bound to become profoundly affected by the breakdown of the East–West dualism of international politics and the revolutionary changes in eastern and central Europe in the last decade of that century.

While the reemergence and ascendancy of liberal and socialist internationalism in Western Europe during the cold war had been on the whole a slow and gradual process, the retreat of conservative internationalism and the advance of liberal and, to a lesser extent, of social democratic internationalism in most of Europe in the early 1990s were quite sudden developments. The end of the cold war and the collapse of the Soviet Union, soon made a form of internationalism that focused primarily on threats to security and peace in the existing or foreseeable situation seem less relevant to the problems and opportunities at hand. The same events very quickly presented new openings for the more optimistic and progressive types of internationalism. For social democrats, the breakdown of communist governments and reorganization of central and eastern Europe offered fresh opportunities to pursue their economic, social and administrative goals through a widening and deepening of the EU, and to establish new transnational links with countries formerly closed to them. For liberals, the revolutionary events throughout the region formerly known as Eastern Europe meant a dramatic enlargement of their sphere of political and economic influence. While several of the new, postcommunist governments embraced long-established liberal ideas of parliamentary democracy, market economy, free trade and international organization, the disintegration of the Soviet Union and Yugoslavia and war and civil war in the Balkans called for a revival of certain liberal doctrines that had been largely dormant in the period of the cold war, in particular those of national self-determination and humanitarian intervention.

But, though the post–cold war transformation of the European political landscape was in many ways highly propitious for the more progressive traditions of internationalism, it also provided encouragement for certain ideological tendencies that were hostile to such internationalism. The convulsions in various parts of Europe not only gave free rein to some types of nationalism, which were already quite active, but also tended to revive others that had been largely repressed in the years of East–West tension and Soviet regional hegemony.

PART II

Nationalism

Table 4 Conservative Nationalism

Type	Roots	Characteristics	Concerns and goals	Ascendancy	Exponents	Modern manifestations
Defensive	European states system of 16th, 17th and 18th centuries French Revolution and Napoleonic Wars Political realism Concept of nationality	Against: conservative solidarism and progressive forms of internationalism For: national sovereignty and existing international order State-nation centered	National interests, rights and values Security	Later part of 19th century Second half of 20th century	Canning Disraeli de Gaulle Thatcher	Opposition to: Pressure from superpowers Threat from major powers Supranational tendencies of ECSC and EEC/ EC/EU
Aggressive		Liberation from alien rule Exclusion of minorities Territorial revision Tendencies toward imperialism Elements of fascism Resort to violence	Independence or aggrandizement Survival or hegemony	Pre-1914 decades Interwar period Last decade of 20th century	Hitler Milosevic Zhirinovsky	Insurrections, civil wars and wars in former Yugoslavia and former USSR Persecution of minorities

Table 5 Liberal Nationalism

Type	Roots	Characteristics	Concerns and goals	Ascendancy	Exponents	Modern manifestations
Defensive	Revolutionary and Napoleonic Wars Marriage of liberalism and nationalism: liberal democracy and national self-determination	Against: pluralist and solidarist conservative, social democratic and communist internationalisms For: individual and national rights Nation- and people-centered Middle class	Distinct identity and separate existence of nation Domestic progress	19th century 1919 1990s	Mazzini Michelet J. S. Mill Havel	Opposition to: Superpower hegemony or primacy Aspects of NATO policy Federalist tendencies of European Communities
Aggressive		National liberation, unification or integration Tension between liberal and nationalist elements Shift from liberalism toward nationalism Passionate and assertive	Independence Unity Power	Later part of 19th century 1990s	Droysen Treitschke	Uprisings, secessions and wars in former Yugoslavia and former USSR

Table 6 Socialist Nationalism

Type	Roots	Characteristics	Concerns and goals	Ascendancy	Exponents	Modern manifestations
Communist	*USSR:* Socialist reactions to WWI Lenin's theories Stalin's policies Emergence of USSR as great power "Great patriotic war" *Eastern Europe:* Establishment of Tito's Yugoslavia and people's democracies *Western Europe:* Soviet control of communist parties	*USSR:* "Socialism in one country" Soviet hegemony *Eastern Europe:* Reaction to Soviet socialist internationalism Defensive and governmental *Western Europe:* Growing dissatisfaction with Soviet control of communist parties	*USSR:* Serve own needs Control Socialist Commonwealth *Eastern Europe:* Protect rights of states and interests of régimes *Western Europe:* Reduce dependence on Moscow Gain recognition for national characteristics	*USSR:* WWII Cold war *Eastern Europe:* Post-Stalin period of cold war *Western Europe:* Later decades of cold war	Stalin Tito Ceaucesco	*USSR:* Soviet imperialism *Eastern Europe:* Conflict or tensions with USSR *Western Europe:* Estrangement from Moscow Eurocommunism Break-away parties

Table 6 Continued

Type	Roots	Characteristics	Concerns and goals	Ascendancy	Exponents	Modern manifestations
Social democratic	Non-Marxist socialism in 19th century Revisionist Marxist socialism in pre-1914 decade Recognition of usefulness of state Experience or prospect of governmental office	Against: conservative and liberal internationalism For: national pursuit of economic and social programs People-centered Working class	Protection for social achievements Equality and welfare through legislation	Cold war	Papandreou Palme	Opposition to: Leadership and policies of NATO Goals and programs of ECSC and EEC/EC
Socialist	Disillusion with Soviet communism in later 1950s East–West détente in 1960s	Against: conservative and liberal internationalism For: traditional socialism, environmental concerns and peace movements Anti-American Pro-Third World Radical style	Egalitarian social order Environmental protection Détente and peace	1960s, 1970s and 1980s	Larsen	Opposition to: NATO and EC US policies Superpower rivalry

CHAPTER 4

Conservative Nationalism

L ike its internationalist counterpart, the primary form of European nationalism is derived from the conservative trend of thought about international politics. Typically motivated by a desire to maintain existing structures and uphold traditional values, conservative nationalism, particularly in its modern appearance, has often been directed against programs and achievements of the two more progressive forms of internationalism. With conservative internationalism, however, it has not necessarily been in conflict. In some situations the two have actually complemented each other.

Origins and Development

The conservative pattern of international thought goes back almost to the time when European states established themselves and began to interact politically. They emerged after the disintegration of medieval unity, which had been characterized by a complex distribution of power among a large number of units and shaped by centuries of cooperation and rivalry between emperors and popes. Able to meet both the economic and the military challenges of the time, the new states soon secured legal and political independence. Consolidating their position as the principal political units, they changed the character of European politics. Each of them determined to secure its military and economic position and survive indefinitely, they engaged each other in a competition for territory and rivalry for power. Thus, the politics of Europe became distinguished by continual conflict and shifting alliances among sovereign states, and its history marked by wars and peace settlements.

Through the competitive pursuit of state interests, the population of each power involved in the rivalry tended to develop an emotional force that may be seen as a forerunner of modern nationalism. A mixture of collective patriotism for the country and popular loyalty to the ruler, it had a territorial base and a dynastic focus. Early in the sixteenth century it was already strong enough for Machiavelli to describe it as a "civic religion." Over the next few centuries such rudimentary nationalism remained a force of some significance in regional and European politics. While serving to strengthen each state in its interaction with others, it may also have played some part in inciting antagonism and accentuating conflict between the powers.

But it was not till after the French Revolution that nationalism emerged in its modern European form. Once the word nation became associated with the concept of nationality, in the sense of a people conscious of sharing a historic identity expressed in a common language, nationalism came to mean the collective self-assertion of such nationality. Between the Revolutionary and Napoleonic Wars and WWII the new nationalism was a growing force in European politics. It inspired the independence of small states, the unification of great powers and the break up of empires. While it roused suppressed peoples and invigorated old nations, it also brought a new passion to international relations. Intensifying crises and wars, it complicated the management of international politics. In intention as in effect, it challenged and checked the principles and practices of various kinds of internationalism.

Not all such nationalism, however, was of a conservative kind. With the new political ideologies that gained support in that period of European history came two other forms of nationalism. While the rise of liberalism in the earlier part of the period brought with it the development of a liberal form of nationalism, the spread of socialism in the later part led to the emergence of various types of socialist nationalism. Yet, though at times overshadowed by prevailing versions of internationalism or rivaling kinds of nationalism, conservative nationalism was nearly always a force of some significance. Even in the post-Napoleonic decades, which were dominated by two types of conservative internationalism, some influence was exercised by conservative nationalism. Some of it was directed against the solidarist conservatism and interventionist policies of the powers of the Holy Alliance, and some against the pluralist conservatism and balance-of-power praxis of the Concert of Europe. Though liberal nationalism often prevailed in the middle decades of the century, in some countries it was soon eclipsed by a conservative nationalism that eventually, during the decades leading up to 1914, was transformed into imperialism.

The interwar period started as an age of internationalism, in particular of the liberal and socialist kinds, but soon saw the rise of extreme rightist versions of conservative nationalism, in the shape of fascism and nazism. The second half of the twentieth century brought a revival of various types of conservative nationalism. Initially largely a reaction to the forms of internationalism that prevailed in the first postwar decades, more recently that development was facilitated and conditioned by the elimination of the communist version of socialist internationalism.

Like its internationalist counterpart, conservative nationalism in modern Europe typically reflected a rather pessimistic view of human nature, politics and history. It tended to be realist, in the sense of presenting international society as a multiplicity of sovereign states engaged in a competitive interaction that was marked by continual conflict and occasional war. It was state-centered, accepting the powers of Europe as the fundamental political units and assuming that each of them was motivated largely by self-interest. Its basic themes, too, were much the same as those of conservative internationalism, namely the pursuit of security and, ultimately, the struggle for survival. The difference lay in the means it prescribed and the programs it offered.

Conservative nationalism tended to be not only egocentric in character but also retrospective in orientation. It drew its inspiration largely from notions and images of the nation's past, and only rarely from projections for the future of international society. Its picture of the past, however, could be highly selective, and might comprise mythical elements drawn from the earliest periods of national history as well as parts based on achievements accomplished and experience gained in more recent times. The attachment to the history and culture of the nation could be of a moderate and reasonable kind, or it could be more extreme and fanatical. The policies and programs expressing such nationalism might be essentially defensive, or they might be of a decidedly aggressive nature. Such differences of quality were already apparent in the nineteenth-century development of conservative nationalism in particular countries.

Germany

The German tradition of conservative nationalism had its roots in two intellectual movements that gained political influence in the later years of Napoleonic rule and the first period of post-Napoleonic restoration. One was a romanticism of deep and dark forces, the other a political philosophy of hard and self-regarding doctrines. Initially neither of them was a national political force. Though German romanticism was nationalist, it was in its earliest stage hardly a political movement. While Hegelian thought was political, it was for a long time not nationalist. But as the two developed and eventually merged, with each other and with various other intellectual and emotional trends, they became the most powerful and lasting influence in German politics of the late nineteenth and early twentieth centuries.

Romanticism, in European intellectual history largely a reaction to the rationalism of the Enlightenment, started in Germany as essentially a cultural movement. Exemplified by the writings of Adam Müller, it rejected the liberal values of Western civilization and praised the unique past of the German nation, without presenting an explicit political program. For Müller as for Fichte, the national goal was a "fatherland of the mind," not the integrated state or the new great power that became the preoccupation of later generations. Other influential writers, notably Ernst Moritz Arndt and Friedrich Ludwig Jahn, added a political dimension to early romanticism. Focusing on the Middle Ages, which they regarded as the original source of national culture, they discovered the mystical forces of race and language, *Volk* and God, which in their view made the German nation not merely unique but superior to all other nations. Sharpening the edge of romantic nationalism, they turned it against France in particular and Western influences in general and called for active resistance to alien rule.

The political side of Hegelian thought was conservative in the most realist sense of the term. It venerated the state, focused on its power and interests and accepted war as an essential part of its relations with other states. For Hegel and his disciples, the states of Europe were in a state of nature, all engaged in a continual struggle for survival. But nationalism was not a part of their ideology. Though Hegel keenly desired a strong Germany, he did not expect its reorganization to come about as a result of the efforts of the people, but through the will of a strong leader. His political philosophy owed little to the ideas of 1789 and the influences of the French Revolution and much to the principles and practices of Napoleon, whom he admired. Highlighting state egotism, Hegelian ideology was opposed to all kinds of internationalism, even the conservative internationalism during 1815–48.

In the Restoration period the ideological debate in Germany was largely between those who subscribed to the solidarist internationalism of the Holy Alliance or the pluralist internationalism of the Congress system and the European Concert and those who opposed such conservative internationalism. The latter consisted mainly of moderate constitutionalists in the secondary states of the Confederation, radical liberals in the smaller states, national liberals in Prussia and revolutionaries wherever they were. Conservative nationalism was not a significant influence in this debate.

The ascent of such nationalism came half a century after the peace settlement of 1815 and the establishment of the German Confederation, when German liberalism had gone into decline and Bismarck had taken charge of Prussian politics. The drive toward national unification and German hegemony in the 1860s and 1870s may be seen as motivated mainly by the two intellectual and emotional forces introduced earlier, namely a surviving and long since politicized romanticism of the self-absorbed and self-glorifying kind and a revived and nationalized realism of a particularly egotistical and ruthless type. The establishment of the German *Reich* consolidated the merging of the two constituent strands of conservative nationalism. But, in Bismarck's European policies after 1871, very much of the realist mold, German nationalism was usually checked by a measure of conservative internationalism. After his demise, however, that internationalism was soon inundated by the great confluence of nationalist thought that took place toward the end of the century. The nationalism of conservatives merged with the nationalism of national liberals, themselves strongly influenced by Hegelian doctrines and attitudes, and became part of the imperialist ideology that fired public opinion and dominated the foreign policy of Germany in the years before WWI.[1]

Although the imperialism of *Weltpolitik* led Germany to war and defeat, that did not put an end to the conservative tradition of German nationalism. In the revolutionary mood after 1918, such nationalism took a turn to the right and became one of the forces that helped to undermine the Weimar republic. Both its romantic and its realist elements were accentuated. There was a revival of the mysticism that had characterized the first generation of German nationalism in the nineteenth century as well as a new emphasis on the Hegelian concepts of state, power and war. In both of its aspects, the nationalism of the 1920s showed a complete confidence in the superiority of Germany and a haughty disdain for the Western countries.[2]

In the 1930s Hitler and the National Socialist Party took the development to its most extreme point. Vulgarizing the conservatism of generations of intellectuals, they initiated a program based on the purity of the German race and the superiority of the German state. Inspired by Teutonic myths, guided by deep-rooted racism and stirred by Prussian militarism, they launched Germany on its historic mission of uniting all German lands and reorganizing international society. Their plan was to conquer Europe and replace the states system with a hierarchical structure based on racial distinctions. While the Aryans would be placed at the top and various other races relegated to lower levels, individuals and races deemed subhuman would be exterminated.

France and Britain

The French and British trends of conservative nationalism may be dealt with more briefly. Neither of them went to such extremes, or became so powerful an influence in European politics, as the Germans. Yet, in broad terms, the development of each took a course not very different from that of Germany. In the later part of the nineteenth century, when liberal nationalism was declining in both countries, conservative nationalism was on the rise. The ascent of the latter was again accompanied by an accentuation of its realist qualities and a bent toward turning itself into imperialism. Moreover, as in Germany, there was a tendency in each country for conservative nationalism to go beyond its nature of largely an intellectual trend and become more of a popular movement. Such similarities suggest that the ideological development within each of the three countries was not merely a result of national influences but also a reflection of wider cultural, social and intellectual forces at work in Europe in the late nineteenth and early twentieth centuries.

Invigorated by the Napoleonic experience of national self-assertion through conquest and domination, conservative nationalism in post-1815 France was fortified by the restoration of the Bourbon monarchy, the signing of the Quadruple Alliance of the victorious great powers and the introduction of the congress system of European diplomacy. But the July revolution of 1830, which signaled a revival of liberalism, proved to be a setback for conservative thought. The events of 1870–1, however, led to a reversal of the fortunes of the liberal and the conservative trend. After the Franco-Prussian War and the failure of the Paris Commune liberal nationalism soon became less liberal, eventually losing its identity as a political force. Following the military defeat of France, the Bismarckian unification of Germany and the establishment of the new *Reich*, conservative nationalism grew more extreme, grandiose and strident.

Championing rightist, royalist, anti-parliamentary and eventually also anti-Semitic ideas, writers such as Charles Maurras and Maurice Barrès revealed fascist inclinations in their thoughts about national politics. Their writings about foreign policy, which focused on the past grandeur of the nation and its future role in the world, manifested ever-stronger imperialistic qualities. In the last decades before 1914 such nationalism found expression in the pages of a new periodical, *Action Française*, as well as in the activities of a political movement. Though not so powerful as the fascist movements of postwar Italy and Germany, the latter pursued its goals largely by similar means, deploying violent street gangs and other forms of populist intimidation. Highlighting the themes of national unity, greatness and glory and adopting a brutal style of campaigning, the new version of conservative nationalism drew its support from the lower middle class rather than from the intelligentsia. It survived WWI and became a substantial influence in French politics in the interwar period.

British conservative internationalism in the post-Napoleonic period of quadruple alliance and congress diplomacy provoked critical reactions from several quarters that, for one reason or another, were opposed to the Metternichian policies of joint intervention and concerned about British involvement in Continental politics. Some of the criticism came from within the governing Tory Party itself and, in signal cases, revealed the presence of a conservative form of nationalism. The most prominent example was that of George Canning. Opposing the dynastic dogma of antirevolutionary intervention, "the doctrine of an European police" as he called it, and dissociating himself from the "areopagitical spirit" of the Continental allies, he championed the principle of nonintervention and repudiated the entire system of diplomacy by congress. After becoming foreign secretary, he did more than any other man in Europe to put an end to that system. His declared aim was to extricate Britain from unnecessary European involvement and restore its independence—"for Europe . . . now and then to read England."[3] That kind of nationalism remained one of the ideological influences behind the tendency to stay aloof from Continental politics, which much of the time characterized British foreign policy during the next half century.

Conservative nationalism in nineteenth-century Britain reached its most advanced form in the years between the Congress of Berlin and WWI. At that stage of its development it was largely a reaction to liberal internationalism, which was then establishing itself as Britain's principal tradition of thought about European politics. Conservative thought was opposed to the ideas of humanitarian intervention, which characterized the earlier phase of that tradition of internationalism, as well as to the concept of international organization, which marked its later phase. Against such progressive notions it set the traditional principle of security of states through balance of power. Often the conservative concern for British national interests revealed nationalist tendencies, which in the later part of the period usually took the form of imperialism. The principal representative of this way of thinking was Disraeli. Inclined, with Canning, for Europe to read England, he appealed to the people to set aside the cosmopolitan principles of liberalism and embrace the national ideas. Wanting European policies and Continental involvement to be restricted to the application of the principles of the balance of power, he looked beyond Europe and focused on the power and prestige of the Empire in the world. Enjoining Britain to keep a "proud reserve" from Europe and pursue its interests in the world, the nationalism of Disraeli and his disciples in the 1870s and 1880s led to the conservative imperialism of the next decades.[4]

During and immediately after WWI, when the principle of national self-determination was being canvassed throughout much of Europe and the territorial part of the Versailles settlement was being prepared, liberal nationalism, which in the later part of the century before 1914 had been largely eclipsed by liberal internationalism, had a revival in British thought about European politics. The establishment of the League of Nations, however, marked a shift back toward the kind of liberal internationalism that had prevailed in the prewar decades. But soon conservative nationalism and imperialism reasserted themselves in British official thinking. Thus, the ideological conflict became again, as before the war, between the liberal doctrine of international organization and the conservative principle of extra-European interests and responsibilities, though with the latter now having the advantage.

The nationalism and imperialism of British conservatives, however, no longer rested on a watchful concern about the balance of power in Europe, as they had done in Disraeli's days. Rather, the new ideological trend involved a certain lack of attention to European politics. In the 1920s, most conservative nationalists, like so many other people, tended to assume that the new system of collective security, as enshrined in the Covenant of the League and applied in the Locarno treaties of 1925 guaranteeing the Franco-German frontier, had disposed of old-fashioned power-political conflicts in European international relations. In the 1930s they were distinctly reluctant to engage themselves in the increasingly difficult and dangerous situation that was developing on the Continent. Such attitudes were reinforced through the influence of the conservative press. Though the British newspapers of the time rarely went to such extremes as the French, quite a few of which took ultra-rightist and even fascist positions, many of them expressed a narrow and insular form of conservative nationalism. While some newspapers took a rather sympathetic view of Hitler and his entourage, others showed relatively little interest in political events and developments on the Continent.[5] Thus, almost till the eve of WWII the British government and population, the latter still under the shadow of WWI losses, were neither physically prepared nor mentally inclined to intervene forcefully in European politics and help check the aggressions of the fascist powers.

Though initially often a reaction to conservative or liberal internationalism, nineteenth- and early twentieth-century conservative nationalism soon established itself as an autonomous force in each of the major European countries. In the later part of the period it generally transformed itself into an imperialism which, in some Continental countries, eventually became fascist and, in Britain, took an isolationist form. After the middle of the century, when the fascist powers in central and southern Europe had been defeated and the imperialist powers in western Europe had been dwarfed by the emergence of the superpowers of the West and the East and challenged by the anticolonialism of the Third World, conservative nationalism in Europe took new forms.

Modern Forms

Most conservative nationalism in the half century after WWII was primarily of a defensive kind. Evolved to protect national interests, rights and values, it was directed against a wide variety of external threats. Some perceived menaces took the form of economic, political or military pressures from a superpower or a major European power. Other threats came from the principal international organizations of the region, whether the military alliances or the political and economic institutions. Since most of the adverse influences and potential challenges of such powers and organizations were presented in the name of one form or another of internationalism, conservative nationalism often appeared as a reaction to a prevailing internationalism. Some conservative nationalism, however, was of a more aggressive and self-assertive kind, typically appearing in defiance of an alien government or as a challenge to a neighboring state. While defensive nationalism was more common in the four decades of cold war, aggressive nationalism was rife in the years after the decline of East–West conflict in European politics.

Whether of one kind or the other, conservative nationalism usually had several elements, presenting political, economic and cultural aspects. In each case, the semblance of the phenomenon depended largely on the nature of the threats perceived and the goals set by the nationalists. While some nationalism was largely political, others were more economic or cultural. Here the focus will be mainly on the sort of conservative nationalism that found political expression and made an impact on the international relations of Europe.

In the earlier decades of the period, the most prominent and influential conservative nationalist in Western Europe was Charles de Gaulle. Since his youth he had entertained mystical ideas of the nature and role of his country. Likening it to the princess in fairy tales or the Madonna in frescoes, he had imagined France as "dedicated to an exalted and exceptional destiny" and convinced himself that it could not really be itself unless it was in the front rank. France, he had concluded, "cannot be France without greatness."[6]

Inspired by such exalted views, he had developed a political philosophy that focused on the power and independence of the state.

In his foreign policies de Gaulle concentrated almost exclusively on the national interests and prestige of France. After the end of WWII, until he left office in 1946, he strenuously opposed the federalist tendencies in Western Europe and resisted the American influence in European politics, both of which he perceived as challenges to French sovereign rights and national interests. Later, in his postwar *Memoirs*, he launched a bitter attack on his successors in office, complaining that they had immediately jeopardized everything he had accomplished "as regards the independence, the status and the interests of France." In the name of European unity, the new régime had liquidated the advantages gained through victory in the war and, on the pretext of Atlantic solidarity, had subjected France to an Anglo-Saxon hegemony.[7] From his return to office in 1958 till his retirement in 1969 he adhered to his policies of checking federalist tendencies in Western Europe and opposing "Anglo-Saxon hegemony" in the Western alliance.

In his criticism of the structure of the ECSC and the development of the EEC, de Gaulle opposed the supranational efforts of the Eurocrats and advocated a more traditional approach to international organization. But his reaction to "Community Europe" was also motivated by a long-standing suspicion of American policies and influence in Europe. At a press conference in May 1962, he spoke sarcastically about a "so-called integrated Europe," which would have no policy of its own and would come to depend on someone outside, someone who would have a policy. "There would perhaps be a federator, but it would not be European."[8] His issue with the EEC reached a climax in 1965. Provoked by the determined efforts of Walter Hallstein, Adenauer's confidant and the first president of the Commission, to expand the supranational role of this body and speed up the process of economic integration, he suspended French participation in all EEC activities and demanded radical revision of the Treaty of Rome. But in the ensuing confrontation with the leaders of the other EEC members, who included such dedicated Europeanists as Joseph Luns of Holland and Paul Henri Spaak of Belgium, he eventually had to back down and abandon his attempt to have important treaty commitments abrogated.

De Gaulle's animosity toward international integration and commitment to French independence were manifested even more forcefully in his alliance and security policy. Here his old prejudice against the Anglo-Saxon nations, which had been deepened by wartime resentments about his years in London and postwar suspicions of former allies, found expression in a determined opposition to what he regarded as an Anglo-Saxon hegemony within the

Western alliance system. To break that hegemony within NATO became his first diplomatic goal. Initially he proposed a tripartite form of organization according to which the United States, Britain and France jointly would control strategic decision-making on a global basis. When he could not have that, he first detached French forces from the military integration of the alliance and subsequently pursued a policy of reduced participation in NATO activities in general, until he finally withdrew France from the military side of the alliance and expelled all NATO elements from French territory.

Directed against the two principal threats to the independence of France, namely the EEC and NATO, de Gaulle's nationalism was motivated by a concern for national sovereignty, and ultimately for the survival of France as a great power in a world of sovereign states. As we have seen, this form of nationalism went hand in hand with a conservative internationalism, the political program of which was to construct a new Europe that, stretching from the Atlantic to the Urals, and under the leadership of France in the West, would be strong enough to play the role of balancer "between the two New Worlds."

In the later part of the period, one of the most outstanding exponents of conservative nationalism was Margaret Thatcher, who dominated British politics from the late 1970s to the early 1990s. In her foreign policy she was in several ways quite different from de Gaulle. In the first place, her primary interests and expertise were not at all, and especially not in her first years of office, in foreign affairs but in domestic politics. Nor did she harbor any great vision for Europe. Compared with many other British politicians of her time, she was always distinctly anti-European. In her policy toward the West in general, she also took a different line from de Gaulle, leaning heavily on the United States and playing a full and active part within NATO. In her opposition to the Eurocratic drive toward a united Europe and her defense of sovereign rights, interests and values, however, she had much in common with her French predecessor.

Sharing few of the ideas and goals of the Eurocrats, Thatcher generally disliked the policies and processes of Brussels. Not attracted by the corporatist principles that had inspired the founders of the European Communities and strongly opposed to the socialist doctrines that guided some later Europeanists, she could not support the cause of European unity. The idea of a European union, which by the 1980s could be seen as a product of conservative solidarism and socialist internationalism, she rejected as "airy-fairy." Suspicious of the cozy "Euro Club" and temperamentally reluctant to compromise, she resisted tendencies toward supranationality and opposed the processes of consensus. Her inclination to discuss EC issues in terms of "them" and "us" indicated her general attitude to the Continental partners.

What Margaret Thatcher feared was the emergence of a European super-state that "submerges our identity and snuffs out our sovereignty." She wanted Britain to continue with all its rights, interests and values, as she saw them, intact. Her moral commitment to national succession, as deep and instinctive as de Gaulle's, was buttressed by a set of notions of the distinct-ness of Britain. One was the idea of separateness, of ultimately standing alone in times of crisis, in the spirit of Dunkirk. In May 1989 she told Parliament that England must remain "free in order to save Europe again in the case of war." Another idea was that of uniqueness, of having institutions and prin-ciples infinitely better than those of other countries, a frequent theme of Thatcher's speeches. A third notion was of British superiority of character and gift for leadership, of having a special role to play in Europe. Despite the fact of French leadership in the 1970s and the prospect of German superior-ity in the future, the expectation of a leading role for Britain remained part of Thatcher's European outlook in the 1980s. In championing national rights, interests and values, Thatcher, like most nationalists, often resorted to emotive language and deliberate exaggerations. The war over the Falkland Islands marked a high point of nationalist self-indulgence.

The ardent nationalism in her policies toward Europe was complemented by a mild internationalism, which was of a liberal rather than a conservative kind. In the tradition of the Manchester School, she believed in the free play of market forces. Unfettered by tariffs and other forms of governmental interference, commerce and production would provide maximum benefits for all parts of Europe and every section of society. Thus, she supported the drive for a single European market, and signed the Single European Act of 1986. While her goals for the EC could be summarized as a common mar-ket and weak institutions, her message for Eastern Europe was capitalism and democracy.

In extra-European affairs, Margaret Thatcher's nationalism was tempered with an internationalism that was more conservative than her European internationalism. Eager to stem the decline of British influence in interna-tional politics and anxious to play a major role in East–West relations, she engaged Britain in power politics at the regional as well as the global level. In both spheres she leaned heavily on the United States. Finding herself in ide-ological agreement with Ronald Reagan, she championed and developed the "special relationship" between the two principal English-speaking powers. Under her leadership, Britain played a full part in both the diplomatic and the military activities of NATO, and engaged deeply in the Gulf War.

Even her attitude to the Commonwealth, which she sometimes referred to as "their club," was a mixture of internationalism and nationalism.[9]

Conservative nationalism of the anti-American, anti-NATO or anti-EEC kind went beyond the two major West European powers and also gained a certain influence in some small states in the region. Greek politics in particular were at various stages dominated by passionate anti-American and anti-NATO feelings. After the fall of the Colonels' régime, the foremost exponent of such nationalism was Constantine Karamanlis, who in 1974 had returned to Greece to form a democratic government. The nationalist statements and actions that characterized his policies in the following years, however, expressed the feelings of the Greek people rather than his own convictions. Karamanlis himself had for long been an internationalist of markedly Western orientation. As such, he had been selected by the King in 1955 to succeed Marshal Papagos as leader of the rightist Greek Rally, which the following year was reorganized as the National Radical Union (ERE). As prime minister during 1955–63, he had occasionally been accused by opponents and critics within Greece of betraying the cause of Hellenism in the interests of NATO and the Americans. In the same years he had started negotiations for associate membership of the EEC, largely in order to protect Greece against the neutralist tendencies of the opposition parties.

After the restoration of democracy in 1974, however, Karamanlis had to check his pro-American inclinations and give voice to Greek nationalism. Across the political spectrum there was a strong feeling against the United States for having tolerated, and perhaps covertly supported, the military régime, and against NATO for having failed to prevent the Turkish invasion and occupation of part of Cyprus, public bitterness focusing on Henry Kissinger and the Central Intelligence Agency (CIA). In that situation, the relatively mild type of measures that in various political crises in the 1950s had proved adequate to appease public opinion would not do. As an appropriate protest against US policy and NATO attitudes, Karamanlis decided to withdraw the Greek armed forces from the integrated military command structure of NATO, put an end to certain US military and naval facilities and, in general, question the future of American bases on Greek soil. Despite his nationalist policies toward the United States and NATO Karamanlis remained essentially pro-Western. Partly to compensate for the breach with NATO and the strained relations with the Americans, he concentrated his efforts on negotiating full membership of the EEC.

According to reports, Karamanlis on one occasion during those critical years remarked privately that he was the Americans' only friend in Greece but dared not admit it.[10] The nationalist feelings that he felt compelled to express were directed against the alliance and the alliance leader, though ultimately, of course, induced by fear of and animosity toward Greece's neighbor and historic enemy. But it was a nationalism that looked toward the West, in particular Western Europe, and rejected the idea of a purely Balkan identity for Greece. Its basic elements were, as usually in modern Greece, the Greek language, Orthodox religion and a keen awareness of classical greatness. In the right-of-center nationalism of New Democracy, the party Karamanlis had set up to take the place of the pre-coup ERE, there was also at that stage a certain amount of royalism.

After the end of the cold war, the collapse of the Soviet Union and the breakup of Yugoslavia, various parts of Europe saw a revival of a nationalism that had been more characteristic of some earlier periods of European history than of the age of East–West rivalry. More than a reaction to supranational tendencies in European integration or superpower influence in regional politics, it was directed against neighboring states or peoples and aimed at local or regional domination. A prominent exponent of this more aggressive form of nationalism was Vladimir V. Zhirinovsky in Russia. As leader of the Liberal Democratic Party, which came into being in 1990 and received nearly a quarter of the votes in the election in December 1993, he vowed to "bring Russia up off its knees." His political program, which was couched in bombastic language, appeared to be naked imperialism. His first aim was to restore Russia's former borders, which meant reestablishing domination over the former Soviet republics. Beyond that he talked about reclaiming East Germany, and threatened to "nuke" Japan in response to its claim for a return of the South Kurile Islands seized by the Soviet Union in 1945. The United States he called "the evil empire." At home, he vowed to restore the power of the military industrial complex and planned to purge the country of non-Russians. Like the fascist leaders of the interwar years, he employed his personal charisma and demagogic talents to exploit the frustrations and anger of a population that was experiencing the end of empire, the collapse of social order and the decline of living standards.

Despite the differences of quality and style between a largely defensive and a decidedly aggressive nationalism, all the cases presented here were essentially of the conservative kind. Each rested on realist assumptions about the nature of international society and the needs of the state. Sovereignty and security were the principal concerns.

Influence and Targets

The first years after WWII were not, generally speaking, a time for conservative nationalism. Though the struggle against Nazi expansion and the resistance to German occupation had strengthened nationalism in most parts of Europe, the defeat of Italy and Germany and the change from war to peace had checked all forms of nationalism. In postwar Europe it was widely accepted that nationalist feelings and policies had been the bane of the first half of the twentieth century. While WWI, seen in retrospect, had been a conflict of national self-assertion, WWII had been a result of the nationalist ambitions and aggressive policies of the fascist powers. The crushing of the most aggressive manifestations of conservative nationalism, it was felt, had prepared the way for different trends of thought. Many people in the mid-1940s even believed that the time had come to abandon the traditional concept of sovereign states in favor of some form of international integration.

Nor were the economic and social conditions in those years conducive to a revival of nationalism. Most countries being exhausted, and some devastated, by years of war, few were in a position to entertain extravagant national ambitions. Even the victorious powers had to channel the bulk of national energy into the task of meeting the immediate material needs of their people. Wherever national pride did manifest itself in those years it was usually for the limited purpose of restoring the state and reviving the national economy. Even when such goals had been achieved, most countries found few incentives to turn to any of the traditional kinds of conservative nationalism.

The principal exceptions were the declining imperial powers, notably Britain and France but also smaller states with colonies left. On the right part of the political spectrum of such countries, a conservative nationalism asserted itself, the program of which was to oppose the anticolonial forces of what became known as the Third World and defend the traditional ideas and established possessions of empire. That form of nationalism survived for many years but gradually lost influence, in step with the growing strength and success of the anticolonial movement. In Britain, where decolonization had been undertaken with greater readiness than in France and Portugal, it lasted till well after that process had been largely completed. Remnants of the ideology might be detected in an underlying tendency to identify with Protestant Unionists against Catholic Republicans that often marked British involvement in the conflict in Northern Ireland from the 1970s. A remarkable upsurge of such nationalism in purer form took place in 1982, when a large section of public opinion passionately supported Thatcher's decision to send the Navy to defend the Falkland Islands against Argentine invasion.

Defensive Nationalism

When conservative nationalism did recur in postwar Europe it was not so much a fruit of ideological tradition or a product of social and economic conditions as a reaction to the policies and pressures of the two superpowers.

During most of the cold war the greatest obstacle to a revival of nationalism, particularly of the governmental kind, was the polarization of Europe between the Soviet Union and the United States. But in the earlier part of that period, especially at the stage when the dynamics of dualistic conflict was still in the process of splitting most of Europe into opposite camps, the efforts of each superpower rival to dominate or influence a part of the Continent provoked diverse nationalist reactions in various parts of Europe.

In Eastern Europe, the Moscow-led Communist parties, which shortly after the invasion and occupation by the Red Army secured control of the political life of each country, soon eradicated conservative as well as other forms of "bourgeois" nationalism, which had survived the war. In Bulgaria thousands of nationalists and "fascists" were executed or "liquidated" after the end of hostilities. Later, major trials of army officers and others, including the Agrarian leader Nikolai Petkov who in 1947 was executed for "national treason," were staged to check anti-Russian nationalism. After a plebiscite in 1946, the monarchy was removed and a republic established. At the same time, however, the Russians for purposes of their own tried to manipulate some of the nationalist feelings of Bulgarians by posing as the sponsor of their national interests, particularly in relation to Greek territorial claims. In Hungary the victory of the communists meant the elimination of all remnants of the tradition-bound "feudal" nationalism and the eclipse of other old forms of Magyar nationalism that in earlier years had stood in the way of the communist cause. But here, too, patriotic drives and nationalist sentiments were soon enlisted in support of a program of social restructuring and economic progress along lines laid down in Moscow. In Rumania the destruction of the fascist régime and the liberation by Soviet forces in 1944 seemed to mark the lowest point in the history of Rumanian nationalism. In the following years the new leaders devoted their energy to the pursuit of social revolution in accordance with the precepts of communist internationalism. But later, Rumanian communism reacted to Stalinist and post-Stalinist pressures from Moscow and assumed a more nationalist form, which shared certain of the characteristics usually associated with conservative nationalism. However, since the nationalist tendencies that emerged in Rumania, and eventually also in other people's democracies, pertained to national communism, they come under the heading of socialist nationalism here and are dealt with below.

While the Soviet government and the local Communist parties under its control stamped out all remnants of prewar and wartime conservative nationalism in Eastern Europe, the external and internal threat of communism in Southern Europe rather served to reinforce such nationalism. On the

Iberian peninsula the events in Eastern Europe, the Soviet military and ideological challenge to Western Europe and the potential threat to the political and social order in France and Italy posed by the local Communist parties tended to strengthen the conservative resolve and kindle the nationalist tendencies of the right-wing military dictatorships in Portugal and Spain. This was the case especially in the latter, where memories of the traumatic experience of civil war were still vivid enough to provide a strong incentive to maintain the existing order and suppress all revolutionary tendencies.

In post-1945 Greece the revolutionary efforts of the communists, which were inspired, if not backed, by Moscow and helped from across the borders in the north, led to a confrontation with the government and another round of civil war. The conflict, which polarized the country between the Left and Right, encouraged the latter to develop and defend its ideology. It was markedly nationalist, focusing at first on concerns about national security and the prospect of limited territorial expansion but later also on the ideas and values of Greek-Christian civilization. Conditioned by the cold war and stimulated by fear of communism as well as by a certain amount of Slavophobia, the ideology was pro-Western, and in due course found expression in support for NATO and the West European institutions that emerged in these years. In the decade after the suppression of the communist-led rebellion and the introduction of the Greek Constitution of 1950 the focus of the nationalist ideology of the government and its supporters was on economic, social and cultural development. The conservative nationalism at the heart of that ideology found a more extreme expression in the ideas and program of the Colonels, who committed a *coup d'état* in 1967 and ruled Greece till their régime collapsed seven years later. To some extent too a product of fear of communism within and outside the country, the nationalism of the military dictatorship emphasized the notion of Greece as a nation of Greek Christians with a record of past greatness. As in Franco's Spain, where the army and also the Church were the most powerful institutions, a concern with stability and order was combined with an emphasis on historical grandeur and traditional religious and cultural values.

Although the challenge of communism provoked an ideological response in most parts of Europe, in Western Europe it was not so much communist internationalism directed by the Soviet Union as liberal internationalism championed by the United States that in the later postwar years helped to stimulate a certain reassertion of conservative nationalism. The American drive to integrate Western Europe economically as well as politically, conducted largely through the establishment of the OEEC and the provision of Marshall Aid, was an attempt at radical reconstruction of Europe.

Inspired by the ideas and values of American liberal democracy and guided by the lessons of US history, it was aimed at the creation of some kind of a United States of Europe that could hold its own against the communist part of the Continent. Ultimately such reorganization would mean doing away with the old sovereign nation-states and putting an end to the traditional international politics of Europe.

Pursued in a messianic spirit, the transatlantic liberal internationalist program for the old world met a good deal of resistance from European leaders. Changing combinations of governments opposed most proposals, plans and processes with supranational tendencies. While France and Britain generally played leading parts in the reaction to American pressures, several small countries too, for example Norway, took strong lines to protect their sovereign rights. To some extent, their defense of national rights, interests and values was inspired by conservative forms of nationalism provoked by pressures from the leader of the "free world."

A more constructive European reaction to American economic and diplomatic exertions was to initiate integrative efforts and channel them in other directions. After the late 1940s, when the US drive toward European integration climaxed, Europeans began to develop their own ways of meeting the need for closer cooperation. Having solved their security problem through a military alliance with the two North American powers, they moved toward more exclusively West European responses to the economic and political difficulties that had resulted from WWII and gained salience with the cold war. Instead of the broad and general European institution envisaged by the Americans, six Continental states set up the narrow and specialized ECSC and later initiated other Communities, in particular the EEC. The rest of Western Europe, preferring a much looser structure, formed the EFTA.

The new European organizations, initiated and developed partly as a result of encouragement and partly as a reaction to pressures from the United States, themselves provoked nationalist opposition in Europe. Indeed, the EEC became the principal target of conservative nationalism. The basic reason for the critical reactions to the integrationist tendencies manifested by the new institutions was the particularistic tradition of European politics. In the 1950s, when only a small group of politicians and administrators saw their way to approach international affairs in a European spirit, the majority of people were stuck in the habit of thinking and acting largely within a purely national frame of reference. Accustomed to regard a preoccupation with the sovereign rights, political interests and cultural values of their nation as the highest mark of statesmanship, most politicians had neither the imagination nor the courage to embrace the new ideas and policies. Some of the most determined opposition to supranational tendencies came from leaders of conservative parties.

The Schuman Plan of May 1950 evoked nationalist feelings in several countries, not least Britain. Geographically separated from continental Europe and emotionally linked with the overseas Commonwealth, this country found it hard to accept proposals for a merging of industries under a supranational authority. Harold Macmillan, speaking on behalf of the Conservative Party, declared that "our people will not hand over to any supranational authority the right to close down our pits and our steelworks."[11] In France and Germany, too, the proposals for establishing what became known as the ECSC met with hostile reactions from the Right. For the Gaullists in particular, they amounted to an unacceptable curtailment of French sovereignty. Hostility toward the ex-enemy also played a part in the anti-ECSC campaign of the French Right.

In 1954, when the French government proposed the setting up of a unified European army of small national contingents with a common budget and supranational control, there was another nationalist reaction in France. Rightist critics of the plan were against any limitation of French control of the country's own forces. Together with the communists, the Gaullists defeated the scheme in a parliamentary vote. Later in the decade, when the EEC was established, the principal target of conservative nationalism became the integrationist efforts of the signatories of the Treaty of Rome.

In the 1960s, most anti-EEC nationalism was still directed mainly against the integrationist drives inspired by conservative solidarism. In the following decades, when the movement toward a political union gained fresh momentum and attracted growing support from Social Democratic parties too, such nationalism soon turned against both the traditional solidarist and the new socialist form of European internationalism. Each marked by a measure of Eurocratic *dirigisme*, both forms of internationalism provoked those rightist parties and movements for which national sovereignty remained the overriding concern.

While conservative nationalism in the earlier period was led by de Gaulle's France, in the later decades it was associated more with the British Conservative Party. But, at various stages, it also found exponents and influenced opinion in some smaller European countries. Thus, in the public debate about the EEC in Norway between 1969 and the referendum in 1972, the forces against membership included rightist groups that, in their insistence on national independence, displayed a rather chauvinistic nationalism. Subsequently the new Progress Party maintained an equally nationalistic anti-EEC campaign. In Denmark, too, some of the opposition to the

EEC reflected nationalist attitudes of a conservative brand. Though anti-EEC sentiments were more characteristic of the left and left-of-center parts of the political spectrum, they also marked certain rightist and right-of-center groups and parties both before and after accession in 1973. Danish Rally, a right-of-center party that emerged in the years of occupation and resistance but subsequently went into decline, as well as the Progress Party, a populist protest party with an uneven parliamentary record, exhibited pronounced nationalist inclinations, the former for example in opposing the supranational tendencies within the EEC in the 1960s and the latter by appealing to xenophobic sentiments in the country in the 1980s and 1990s. Commensurate with the multidimensional character of the perceived threat from the various European organs, such nationalism appeared in political and economic as well as cultural forms.

Most conservative nationalism directed against the European institutions, like that targeted at one or other of the superpowers, was essentially reactive and defensive. So was the type of nationalism that was induced by the presence of a preponderant and self-assertive or potentially aggressive state within Europe. The reactions of neighboring countries to developments in the Federal Republic and united Germany sometimes provided examples of that type. The negative response of some French nationalist groups of the far Right to the Schuman Plan in 1950 apparently had its roots not only in traditional hostility toward Germany but also in a growing fear of its potential strength. While one of the causes of early Danish right-of-center opposition to EC membership was a certain amount of lingering anti-German feeling, a major reason for the later anti-EC nationalism of the Progress Party was concern about the overwhelming economic and political power of united Germany. Greece's relations with Turkey presented a less clear example of such nationalism. While not always of a strictly defensive nature, anti-Turkish nationalism on the right of center and far right of its political spectrum generally reflected some concern about the superior power of Turkey and anxiety about its policies and intentions.

Aggressive Nationalism

Apart from Greco-Turkish relations, which at critical junctures usually presented a certain amount of chauvinistic nationalism on both sides, and the hostilities in Northern Ireland, which recurrently evinced the influence of various kinds and degrees of nationalism on the several parties involved, aggressive nationalism was rarely a feature of European politics during the cold war. The polarizing forces of dualistic conflict in global and regional politics tended to suppress nationalist ideas and movements of the more self-assertive and militant type. The first signals of détente in East–West relations in the 1960s, however, were soon followed by early signs of the emergence, here and there, of rightist nationalist ideas, movements and parties of a more radical nature. The programs presented tended to focus on domestic political, economic and social issues and to champion national values of a traditional and rather narrow kind. In Britain, the most interesting case was that of Enoch Powell, a prominent member of the Conservative Party who was hostile to closer links with Europe. When he, in speeches and writings, warned against further immigration and asked for voluntary repatriation of immigrants from other parts of the world he found some public sympathy. In the Federal Republic of Germany the rise, and brief existence, of the National Democratic Party (NPD) in the later 1960s rested largely on a variety of discontents with existing conditions in the Federal Republic in general or in certain *Länder* in particular. The means employed by such movements varied from country to country. While the NPD concentrated on securing parliamentary representation, others, like the National Front in Britain and the black brigades in Italy, habitually resorted to violence.

In the following decades, when the economic conditions of Europe worsened, the target of the extreme right became increasingly immigration. New groups, movements and parties hostile to immigrants, especially those of alien race, emerged in many countries and, despite their narrow membership, helped raise the level of social tension. The most disturbing development was in France, where the National Front under the leadership of Jean-Marie le Pen gained substantial parliamentary representation with an explicitly racist and increasingly also anti-Semitic program. Another new political party of the far right which gained some support by exploiting popular concern about "foreign invasions" was the West German Republican Party. Founded in the 1980s, it presented a program of extreme nationalism, which found most of its supporters in South Germany. By the mid-1990s, however, Europe's strongest nationalist party on the far right was Austria's Freedom Party. Under the leadership of Joerg Haider, who once had praised the employment policies of Hitler and lauded the veterans of the Waffen SS, it gained 28 percent of the votes in the European parliamentary elections in 1996. Tapping dissatisfaction with current austerity measures and growing disillusionment over EU membership, the party presented a program that rejected the Maastricht treaty and called for policies to restrict foreigners and maintain law and order. In other small countries, too, far-right movements with racist programs emerged, but usually with only limited support. In Sweden, which in contrast to Denmark and Norway had no experience of occupation by Nazi Germany, the number of active members of various neo-Nazi groups was in 1999 estimated at about 1000, much more than in the other Nordic countries. The most prominent group was National Socialist Front (NSF), which on the Internet presented a radical racist program embellished with swastikas and Hitler-greetings.

While far-right nationalism in the last few decades of the cold war was aimed largely at internal enemies, namely communists, immigrants, Jews and other groups deemed to present a threat to the established order and traditional values, after the end of East–West conflict and the collapse of communist régimes in Eastern Europe it became directed more at outside opponents, whether minority nationalities or neighboring states. In the early 1990s new, powerful and aggressive forms of conservative nationalism emerged, most of them in southern and eastern Europe. An important part of their program was generally territorial revision. In the former Yugoslavia the Serbs, guided by a particularly virulent nationalism, set out to secure regional domination through conquest. In Greece, the major political parties, New Democracy and PASOK, reacted downright defensively when a small successor state set up on its northern border provoked the nation by calling itself Macedonia, while a new party, Political Spring led by Antonis Samaras, emerged on the Right with a program that carried some hints of territorial expansion at the expense of the offending state. In Russia, Zhirinovsky and his associates in the new Liberal Democratic Party espoused a conservative nationalism that shaded into fascism and imperialism. In some of the other successor states of the Soviet Union, too, right-wing nationalism soon became expansionistic.

Often the new nationalism had a strong religious component. As a determinant of national identity, religion became a salient feature of the ideology of some preponderant nations striving for hegemony as well as of a larger number of lesser nations struggling for survival. It marked the cultural aspect of the post-Soviet nationalism of Russia, and was the distinguishing ideological factor in the post-Yugoslav hostilities between Orthodox, Catholic and Moslem nationalities. Some Greek nationalists of the Right were inclined to make adhesion to the Orthodox faith the criterion of Greekness. Sometimes the religious element in nationalist ideology had a fundamentalist quality, as in recent Turkish nationalism. Usually the presence of a religious dimension in conservative nationalism, whether a case of religionized politics or of politicized religion, signified a degree of fanaticism. It indicated that the struggle was not merely for political security or advantage, but for cultural survival or domination as well.

When viewed in the whole context of European politics since 1945, conservative nationalism may be seen as mainly a series of responses to various forms and manifestations of internationalism. In the earlier decades, it appeared initially as reactions, on the one hand, to the socialist internationalism practiced by the Soviet Union and Western communist parties and, on the other hand, to the liberal internationalism expressed in the European policies of the United States and the programs of certain postwar West European institutions, and subsequently as a response to the solidarist conservative internationalism espoused by the first generation of Eurocrats. In the later decades, it became increasingly a reaction to the socialist internationalism of social democrats and socialists who believed in European centralization and advocated big government through the EC and EU. In both periods, the primary target of conservative nationalism was supranational tendencies, as expressed in the program and policies of the new European institutions.

In the last few decades of the century, some more aggressive kinds of nationalism emerged on the Right or far Right of the political spectra of various countries. Evoked by dangers perceived in domestic affairs or opportunities detected in local international relations, rather than provoked by extra-European political pressures or European integrative tendencies, such nationalism generally asserted itself first in national politics and later in relations with neighboring nationalities. Intensified by faith, fervor and self-sacrifice, it became a powerful factor in generating social conflict and international tension, which sometimes led to civil hostilities and local wars.

As essentially an indirect result of the economic and political restructuring of Europe that started in the postwar decades and continued for the rest of the century, the more reactive type of conservative nationalism pertained to the great debate about reconciliation of national interests and organization of international relations that is still at the heart of modern European politics. The more aggressive types of conservative nationalism, which came with the dissolution of the East–West dynamics of the cold war and gained momentum with the breakup of Yugoslavia and the collapse of the Soviet Union, had to do with urgent questions of rights of peoples, boundaries of states and spheres of influence that were at the heart of the conflicts in southeastern and eastern Europe in the 1990s. While the former type of nationalism put a brake on the process of ordering the affairs of Europe through the integration of states, the latter was a motivating force in the disordering of the Balkans and parts of the former Soviet Union.[12]

CHAPTER 5

Liberal Nationalism

An offspring of liberal thought, the second kind of nationalism distinguished here is of more recent origin than conservative nationalism. Yet, though barely two hundred years old, liberal nationalism has undergone considerable development and appeared in a variety of forms. Generally concerned with the rights, interests and values of nations or nationalities, it has often been directed against the program and achievements of conservative internationalism, especially of the solidarist version, and of socialist internationalism, in particular of the communist variety. With liberal internationalism it has frequently, but not always, gone hand in hand.

Origins and Nature

It was during the Revolutionary and Napoleonic Wars that liberalism and nationalism became linked in European politics. While the Revolutionary armies carried the doctrines of the Enlightenment and the passions of a new popular patriotism to neighboring countries, the Napoleonic invasions brought about the emergence of liberal aspirations and the growth of national sentiments in Germany, Italy, Spain and other occupied territories. The Restoration of 1815 indirectly strengthened the bonds between the two emerging sets of political and social forces. Resting on a dynastic order that had its ideological roots in prerevolutionary Europe and a territorial settlement that took little account of national divisions, the post-1815 structure of Europe offended both liberal beliefs and national feelings, and thus prepared the way for a new political alliance. The emergence of national liberal movements and parties that took place between 1815 and 1848 in various parts of the Continent reflected, on the level of theory, a growing conviction that individual and national rights were complementary and interrelated and, on the level of practical politics, a recognition that the pursuit of civil rights and liberal constitutions had to go hand in hand with the struggle for national independence and self-assertion.

Although nationalism in the nineteenth century, as we have seen, also took other forms, often becoming tied up with conservative ideas, the liberal version became an important influence in the long struggle between the traditional forces of the old Europe and the new cultural, social and political movements of nationally self-conscious peoples. Having established itself as a major element of the ideology of the middle classes in the capitals and other cities of most countries, liberal nationalism played an important part in inspiring revolution against conservative governments, inducing unification of divided nations and bringing about the breakup of multinational empires. While its role in the revolutions of 1830 was limited more or less to the uprisings in Poland and Belgium, its effects in the revolutions of 1848 were more widespread. In the unification of Italy and Germany, it was of decisive importance in the initiation of the process and the definition of the goal, even though other, and less liberal, nationalist ideas and sentiments came to the forefront well before the goal was reached. In the disintegration of the Habsburg and Ottoman empires it was a major force, not least in the politics of the Balkan region in the last decades before 1914.

In WWI, the thinking of some of the leaders of the allied powers was dominated by liberal and national ideas, which was reflected in their plans for the postwar European order. The Versailles peace treaties, though a compromise between different traditions of thought about international politics, introduced a political and territorial order that rested in part on the twin doctrines of democratic government and national self-determination. With the establishment of the League of Nations, however, came a shift of emphasis from the nationalist toward the internationalist element in postwar liberalism. In the triangular ideological conflict that took shape in the later part of the interwar period, liberal nationalism was overshadowed, from one side, by a fascism that was marked by an extreme rightist type of conservative nationalism and, from the other side, by a communism the internationalist element of which was increasingly qualified by a Soviet version of socialist nationalism. Thus, when the dictators defied the Versailles settlement in crises and war, liberal nationalism was a force much too weak to inspire an effective defense of the principles on which it rested.

In the ideological rivalry of the postwar years and the cold-war period, which was largely between different traditions of internationalism, most versions of nationalism were eclipsed, some only partially but others for long periods almost totally. While liberal nationalism was invisible most of the time in the parts of the Continent that were dominated by the Soviet Union, in the rest of Europe it reappeared here and there, but usually only in fairly mild forms. In the beginning it was directed mainly against the superpowers and NATO but later also at the various Communities established in the 1950s. Here the initial target was the solidarist influences and federalist tendencies of a largely conservative nature, which were expressed in the new institutions. Subsequently, however, both the liberal and the social democratic integrationist efforts, too, provoked liberal nationalist reactions in various quarters. In Eastern Europe, the decline of Soviet power and the collapse of communist régimes rapidly led to the rise of an anti-Russian and pro-Western liberal nationalism in some countries. In the former Yugoslavia and the former Soviet Union, the decline of East–West tension and the end of the cold war were soon followed by uprisings, wars and secessions that were partly inspired by various forms of liberal nationalism. In several cases, such nationalism was undoubtedly passionate and aggressive. On the whole, however, liberal nationalism in the second half of the twentieth century was fairly restrained and largely defensive, and in its external aspect directed primarily at institutional pressures and influences that were seen as threats to national rights, interests, values and identity.

Distinguished by a fundamental belief in the free action of individuals, liberal nationalism was, at least in its purer forms, people- and nation- rather than state-centered. At its heart was the concept of a national community that was held together by common memories—of historic achievements as well as of past suffering—and shared values, and sometimes also shared goals. Its earliest expressions often took a literary or cultural rather than an economic or political form. Once such nationalism was manifested politically, it tended to focus on national life rather than on international politics. If, however, an extra-national power presented a challenge or a particular juncture of international politics offered an opportunity, it could turn outwards in defense or pursuit of liberal nationalist values or goals in a wider political context. In the process it sometimes changed character, becoming more ardent and self-assertive. Yet, liberal nationalism, like liberal internationalism, could reasonably be said to rest ultimately on the principle of the primacy of domestic politics.

In its original form, the liberal nationalist philosophy of international politics was based on a theory of harmony, peace and progress. Believing with Mazzini that the nation was "the God-appointed instrument for the welfare of the human race" and that fatherlands were "but workshops of humanity,"[1] many of the early liberal nationalists thought that each nationality ought to form a national state of its own. All states formed in accordance with the national principle, they further believed, would be compatible with each other. Each pursuing its own goals, all of them would live peacefully side-by-side and together contribute to the general progress of humanity. Thus, the doctrine of national self-determination became basic to liberal nationalist thought.

In its domestic aspect resting on the principle of democracy and, in its international aspect, on the doctrine of national self-determination, early liberal nationalism could go hand in hand with liberal internationalism. Both sprang from confidence in the rational and moral qualities of human nature, belief in the harmony of collective interests and faith in the development of national as well as international society. Liberal nationalism, it could be said about this stage of the relationship between the two strands of thought, was conditioned by a complementary internationalism. But that situation did not last. In the course of the nineteenth century, as a growing number of nationalities became politically active and set out on the course toward nationhood, the liberal nationalist tradition became in many places more inclined to throw off the internationalist restraint and abandon some of the old assumptions. Many liberal nationalists gradually recognizing that relations among nations might not always be harmonious, now tended to shift the emphasis in their conception of the nation-state from nation toward state, and eventually to grow more concerned about the power of their state than about the progress of humanity. As a result, some liberal nationalism changed character, becoming more categorical in theory and more aggressive in practice. In extreme cases, it transformed itself into something akin to conservative nationalism of the more assertive kind.

Developments in the Nineteenth and Early Twentieth Centuries

In France, the fatherland of liberal nationalism, the transformation of this tradition of thought was particularly marked. The change, which took place during the century after 1815, was foreshadowed by an equally striking ideological development that was already manifested during the Revolutionary and Napoleonic Wars. No sooner had the Revolution led to war with the conservative powers of Europe than the ideas of freedom and democracy became identified with the defense and survival of France. With Napoleon the national concern shifted to conquest and domination, which were pursued at the expense of the liberal ideals of the Revolution. "La liberté s'était perdue dans la gloire," as Edgar Quinet, a writer who had grown up in the age of Napoleon, put it.[2] Though the defeat of Napoleon put an end to military glory, the restoration of the Bourbon monarchy did not serve to revive faith in French liberalism.

Not till after the revolutions of 1830, which started in Paris and spread east, south and north on the Continent, was it again possible for the French to see their country as the source of liberty for others. In the 1830s and 1840s a new generation of writers emerged who, like their predecessors in the 1790s, fused democratic convictions with patriotism, and projected France in a historic role in the advancement of humanity. Foremost among them was the historian Jules Michelet. In *The History of France*, started within a year of the July Revolution, and in many subsequent books, most notably *The People* published in 1846, he set out his philosophy. It was inspired by devotion to the ideas and sentiments of the French Revolution and faith in the messianic role of France. If only it could unite and find the strength vested in its people, he believed, France could perform a liberalizing mission and speed humanity on its way. His writing and teaching were devoted to awakening France and educating it for its ultimate role as "the glorious pilot of mankind's ship."[3]

Though passionately held, Michelet's nationalism was not of the exclusive and militant type. Strongly opposed to the rational cosmopolitanism of pre-revolutionary Europe, he believed that every modern nation represented an idea worthy of respect. When he gave preeminence to the French nation, it was because he was convinced that the progress of mankind depended on the destiny of France. It was as a future guide or leader of humanity, not as a potential conqueror or oppressor of rivaling powers, that he saw his nation. The role that he assigned to France was in the moral and spiritual sphere of nations rather than in the power-political arena of states. However, Michelet's messianism may be seen as the starting point of a development that led toward a rather less benevolent kind of nationalism.

After the July Revolution, in the times of Adolphe Thiers and Alexis de Toqueville, the prevailing principles of liberal thought about foreign policy were nonintervention and liberal alliances. Most liberalism was of a moderate and cautious kind, which allowed internationalism and nationalism to coexist and complement each other. The events of 1848, however, marked a radicalization of French political thought. The emphasis shifted from nonintervention toward diplomatic pressure and military action in the cause of freedom for suppressed peoples. This development was accompanied by a revival of revolutionary propaganda and expansionistic nationalism, as a result of which the harmonious balance between nationalism and internationalism was upset.

Later in the century, after the Franco-Prussian War and the Paris Commune, the nationalist strand of French liberalism underwent a further transformation. Retaining the passionate quality and aggressive tendencies it had acquired already it became rapidly less liberal. While the focus shifted from people and nation to state and power, themes traditionally associated more with conservative than with liberal thought came to the forefront. Eventually, in a situation in which liberalism almost seemed to have disappeared from the politics of the Third Republic, the remains of liberal nationalism gave way to an unrestrained form of integral nationalism.[4] The latter drew its support more from the lower middle class masses than from the middle-class intelligentsia. Associated in particular with the writings of Charles Maurras and the periodical *Action Française*, this nationalism was royalist and rightist. In contrast with liberal nationalism of the traditional kind, it cultivated the nation-state essentially for the sake of national unity and greatness and with little regard for humanity in general.[5]

The evolution of liberal nationalism in nineteenth-century France broadly reflected, and in turn helped to inspire, the dramatic changes that took place in the political and social life of the country. But it should also be seen in the wider contexts of the intellectual history of Europe and the international politics of the great powers. The decline of the romanticism that in the earlier part of the century animated movements in art and inspired revolutions in politics, and the emergence in the later part of the century of a new realism in science, art and politics also conditioned the nature and course of liberal nationalism in France. A more direct influence on this tradition of thought was the changing quality of European international relations. The transition from congress diplomacy and alliances of liberal powers, which distinguished much of the Restoration period and gave it a rather safe and cozy quality, to the tensions and insecurity associated with the rise of Prussia, the defeat of France and the unification of Germany in the following decades led to a rapid decline of liberal thought. The formation of military alliances and increase in international tension in the subsequent decades, followed by an intensification of imperialist rivalries in the world and a deepening of the divisions in Europe during the period before 1914, created conditions conducive to the rise of non-liberal nationalisms.

Germany

In nineteenth-century Germany, liberal nationalist thought underwent a transformation not unlike that of its French counterpart, but for reasons that, at least in the earlier stages of the process, had to do more with German than with European politics. Before the subjugation of Prussia by Napoleon in 1806–7 there was hardly any nationalism in Germany. Eighteenth-century cosmopolitanism, qualified by loyalty to the sovereign and commitment to the state or city of the locality, still prevailed. Nor was there much democratic liberalism emerging in France and Britain. German liberalism in those years was individualist and spiritual rather than the collectivist and political forms that were establishing themselves in the Western countries. When nationalism did emerge in Germany, in the later years of the Napoleonic upheaval and the first decades of the Restoration period, it took mainly a romantic and conservative form.[6] But in certain parts of Germany, namely the southwest and the Rhineland, another kind of nationalism made a tentative appearance in the years between the War of Liberation against Napoleon and the events of 1848. It was inspired largely by the liberal ideas of Western enlightenment.

This strand of nationalism was associated with Karl von Rotteck and Georg Gottfried Gervinus in particular. Rotteck, who was born in Baden and taught history and political science at the University of Freiburg, had great influence on the post-1815 generation of Germans, not only in his own state but also in two other states that obtained parliamentary institutions in 1819, namely Württemberg and Bavaria. His liberalism was of the Western type, and was directed mainly against the principles of the Holy Alliance and the reactionary policies of the great powers of the European congress system. Having proved his patriotism in the years of Napoleonic rule, he entertained the national idea in the Restoration period. But his nationalism was always second to his liberalism. "I do not desire [national] unity without [political] liberty," he declared in a public speech in 1832, "and I prefer liberty without unity to unity without liberty. I reject unity under the wings of the Prussian or Austrian eagle."[7]

Gervinus, a historian and publicist born in Hessen who spent most of his life at Heidelberg, belonged to a later generation of liberals. Like Rotteck, he championed the principles of constitutional liberalism, and admired in particular the constitution of the United States. As an ardent patriot, he believed that a united Germany could achieve greatness in politics as it had already done in other fields of human endeavor. Organized as a federal union along American lines, it could assume a central role in European politics and, like Britain and the United States, become an example to mankind. In his early years, Gervinus looked to Prussia for German liberty and unity. So he was deeply disappointed by the conservative measures introduced by Frederick William IV in 1847. The following year the National Assembly at Frankfurt, which he had helped to plan, was an even greater disappointment to him. Most of its members turned out to be nationalists rather than liberals, soon giving in to the pressure exerted by the monarchical authorities and the temptations presented by the prospect of national power and public prosperity though Prussian dominance. In southwestern Germany, too, where liberal institutions and democratic movements rapidly collapsed under the force of Prussian invasion and suppression, he saw the conservative forces routing the liberal elements in German politics.

These events spelled the sudden decline and near-extinction of Western liberal influences in German political thought, which had affected some of the smaller states in particular. They also heralded the ascendancy of a form of nationalism that, in its origin and earlier development, was linked with Prussia. Initially inspired by the War of Liberation rather than by the Enlightenment, its adherents called themselves national liberals. Soon, however, they became nationalists more than liberals, in any sense of the latter term. Its leading exponents, in Prussia as well as in the *Reich*, were historians and publicists. Foremost among them were Johann Gustav Droysen and Heinrich von Treitschke.

Droysen, who was born in 1808, held chairs at Kiel, Jena and Berlin in turn and founded the Prussian school of historians. The chief characteristic of this tradition of scholarship, namely the fusion of history and politics by the agency of patriotic passion, marked the writings about German and European politics that he published around the middle of the century. The political system that the great powers had imposed on Europe and Germany in 1815, he wrote in 1848, was "nothing but the artificially shaped head stone of the edifice of international law known as the Holy Alliance, of which the catchwords were legitimacy and the monarchical principle, the goal mutual insurance of princely interests against the so-called revolution, and the constitution, if one can call it that, the *oligarchy of the five great powers*, administered through congresses, conferences, interventions etc." This dual system for Germany and Europe served to guarantee the alleged *juste repartition des forces*, and thus to kill the deepest impulse of the movement for freedom, he went on. It meant that the interpretation of the so-called "interests of Europe" was left in the hands of just those great powers that concerned themselves only with their own advantage and paid the least attention to the rights and freedom of the peoples. Above all, he concluded, Germany was organized and maintained as a political vacuum in the center of Europe.[8]

In Droysen's view, the political and territorial arrangements of 1815 were obsolete. Based as they were on the particularistic organization of Germany, they should be abolished through a reorganization of Germany, a task that could be performed by Prussia. His goal was a united, independent Germany under Hohenzollern leadership. However, the new Germany that he had in mind was not a great power of the traditional dynastic type but a nation-state devoted to securing the prosperity and freedom of the people and maintaining peace and law in Europe. "The time of powers, of dynastic issues, is past; the principle of states, takes their place."[9] In writing off the long-established rule of dynastic powers and projecting the rise of nation-states, Droysen helped to clear the way for the establishment of a tradition of liberal nationalism that, in the second half of the century, became even more closely linked with the financial, political and military power of first the Prussian and then the German state. But, compared with later national liberal writers, he himself did not go very far down that road. Although he, in the situation in 1848, accepted the need for Prussian power, his ambition was to see Germany establish itself as a nation-state rather than as a European power.

Treitschke, too, relied on the resources of the Prussian state for gaining the all-important end of German unification. But for him power was also an end in itself. The starting point of his political thought was the same as Droysen's, namely a national liberal criticism of the Vienna arrangements and the conservative policies of Metternich and his partners. The outcome of the negotiations of the statesmen of 1815 had been a mutilation of Germany and Italy, he complained. Since then, the free life of the European peoples had been suppressed by the police force of the "Vierbunde" of the Holy Alliance powers. Germany, he was convinced, could gain national freedom only by breaking with the particularism of the liberals and princes in the south-German states and taking advantage of the power of Prussia. Saxon by birth and upbringing, Treitschke was passionately pro-Prussian and anti-Austrian. From an early stage he championed the policies that Bismarck later put into practice. Strongly opposed to Western liberalism and the ideas of 1789, he had little difficulty with looking to the Prussian king and his aristocratic chancellor, instead of to the middle classes and the people, for national unification. His liberalism was patriotic rather than democratic.

If the first object of Treitschke's passion was German unification, the second was German power. His reasons for insisting on Germany becoming not merely a nation-state but a power state must be sought in his conception of European politics. To his mind, the natural state of international relations was one of conflict rather than harmony. He did not deny that the states of Europe formed a kind of society, and acknowledged in particular the integrating influences of religion, science and commerce. Even war, he suggested in this context, could be a uniting as well as a dividing element among nations, because "it does not draw them together in enmity only, for through its means they learn to know and to respect each other's peculiar qualities."[10] But it was the separating and disruptive factors of international life that engaged his deeper emotions. With an enthusiasm suggestive of the Hegelians more than of Ranke, Treitschke embraced the idea of struggle. States and war go together, he declared. "Without war no state could be. All those we know of arose through war, and the protection of their members by armed force remains their primary and essential task. War, therefore, will endure to the end of history, as long as there is multiplicity of states."[11] War was not merely unavoidable and necessary but, as a healthy moral and cultural influence on peoples, might also be quite desirable. Given that the life of states was conditioned by continual struggle for survival and recurrent war between great powers, power had to be at a premium. After Prussia's victory over France and Bismarck's establishment of the *Reich*, military power was essential for Germany. Without it, the new state would not be able to defend its position at the center of Europe and secure hegemony on the Continent. While Droysen, who developed his ideas before 1848, would prefer to do away with the oligarchy of great powers, Treitschke accepted the aristocratic order of the states system and supported Bismarck in the drive for European hegemony.

A later generation of writers and scholars continued the transformation of the liberal nationalist tradition. Prominent among them were Friedrich Naumann, a Lutheran pastor and political writer, and Max Weber, the social scientist. Though both of them were guided by a social conscience and liberal views, their primary concern was not with individual rights but with national power. Like so many European intellectuals of their age, they were influenced by social Darwinism. "Learning, culture, custom are of no use whatever in world history if they are not protected and carried by power...." Naumann wrote. "Whoever wants to live must fight. This applies to the individual, to the class, to the nation."[12] Weber too, though skeptical about Bismarck's influence on German history and highly critical of the *Kaiser*, had no doubts about the central importance of the *Machtstaat*.[13]

In the period before WWI, when German foreign policy broke through the European limitations observed by Bismarck and entered the field of *Weltpolitik*, and the great powers engaged each other in a global rivalry of growing intensity, German liberal nationalism soon acquired marked imperialist qualities. Historians and publicists of this tradition of thought supported the new foreign policy of their government as enthusiastically, and stressed the need for state power as strongly, as their predecessors had done under Bismarck. Apart from occasional tributes to the liberal ideal of a harmonious diversity of free nations,[14] their writings about foreign policy, global balance of power and German imperial rule had little to distinguish them from other nationalist and imperialist expressions in pre-1914 Germany.

Like the conservative nationalists, they drew heavily on the concepts and doctrines of Ranke's historiography and Hegel's philosophy, which had been mediated to the German nation by the policies and pronouncements of Bismarck. From Ranke came the doctrine of the primacy of foreign policy and the concept of a European balance of power, which they extended to the world. From Hegel came the notions of the power-state and continual struggle among the great powers, which they again applied to global politics. When the two sets of ideas merged in national liberal nationalism, the Hegelian anti-internationalist influence proved rather stronger than the Rankean conservative internationalism. Any remaining internationalist notions of balance and harmony, whether of conservative or of liberal origin, were overshadowed by nationalist ideas of conflict, power and violence.

Yet, the liberal element, though undoubtedly weakened in the prewar period, remained a part of national liberal thought. It still imbued the distant goal of a global order in which the great powers would be equal and the small nations free. As in previous periods of German history, such liberalism rested on the rights of states and nations and not, as in most west European liberalism, also on the rights of individuals. But it marked off the nationalism of national liberal writers, such as Naumann and the historians Hans Delbrück and Otto Hintze, from that of the conservatives, who tended to focus exclusively on the goal of German supremacy. It was in the policies advocated that there often was little to choose between the two traditions of nationalism. Since the obstacle to equality for the great powers and freedom for the smaller nations in a global balance of power was the hegemony of Britain, the mission of Germany to the world, in the national liberal view, was to challenge Britain, both at sea and in the world beyond the high seas, and seek justice for all nations. Naturally, the prospect of war with Britain made the liberal imperialists focus more on policies in the immediate situation than on distant goals and ideals.

Britain

In contrast with Germany, where a particularistic constitution of thirty-five monarchist states and four city republics frustrated nationalist ambitions for more than fifty years, Britain barely fostered a liberal nationalist tradition of thought in the nineteenth century. Unaffected by the Vienna settlement, its island boundaries could not give rise to a nationalist demand for territorial revision. Yet, sympathy with various European peoples struggling for national statehood did inspire some British criticism of the Restoration principle of permanent boundaries and elicit some support for the patriotic efforts and nationalist ambitions of Continental liberals. Moved by nationalist inclinations, which were at best vicarious, British politicians and writers of such sympathies found it much easier than most of their Continental counterparts to restrain their pursuit of national freedom and to maintain the emphasis on their ultimate goal of individual political liberty.

In the early years of the Restoration period several Whigs, in the House of Commons as well as in the House of Lords, criticized the principles behind the Vienna settlement and attacked the interventionist practices of the three Eastern powers. But, while occasionally accusing the autocratic sovereigns of the Holy Alliance of treating nations as their slaves or attacking the rising liberties of the nations of Europe, they directed their charge at the principles and practices of dynastic rather than of territorial conservatism. Some later Radicals, however, shifted the emphasis from the democratic to the national rights of peoples. Accepting the idea of nationality, they focused on the territorial dimension of the Vienna settlement, and concentrated their attack on the anti-revisionist activities of the powers of the Concert of Europe.

Both the Whig critique of counterrevolutionary intervention and the Radical attack on anti-revisionist policies became elements of the case against the doctrine of the balance of power and the practice of foreign intervention that English Radicals developed in the middle decades of the century. But the argument of these Radicals, as we have seen, formed a major contribution to liberal internationalism, rather than an expression of liberal nationalism. Richard Cobden recognized that the balance of power, as a precept that demanded continual diplomatic meddling and armed intervention, involved the suppression of people struggling for national freedom. But, though a life-long champion of the cause of peoples and nations, he rejected the idea of intervening in the domestic affairs of another state even when it was motivated by a desire to secure the liberation of a nation. As a true internationalist, he believed that the progress of freedom depended more on peace, commerce and education than upon the efforts of cabinets and foreign offices.[15]

One major political philosopher, however, took a rather more interventionist line in his thoughts about European politics and British foreign policy. J. S. Mill, like other Radicals, believed in national as well as democratic freedom. His ultimate aim was free institutions for suppressed peoples. But in general, he thought, a necessary condition for achieving this was "that the boundaries of governments should coincide in the main with those of nationalities." Hence he demanded the right to national independence, and in principle supported policies designed to prevent the liberty of a nation that had risen against its foreign conquerors, from being crushed by tyrannical oppressors. Every liberal government or people, he insisted, had a right to assist struggling liberalism by any reasonable means, including arms. Though neither moved by strong nationalist feelings nor attracted by ideas of a British crusade to liberate peoples on the Continent, Mill played a role in the development of liberal nationalist thought. By stressing the link between democratic freedom and national liberty as political goals and accepting the pairing of constitutionalism and nationalism in the struggles of European liberals, he became one of the fathers of the doctrine of national self-determination, which eventually became a plank of liberal nationalism as well as of liberal internationalism.

The thrust of British liberal thought about European politics was internationalist. When Gladstone and his supporters accepted the idea of nationality, and tried to apply the principle of self-government to the Eastern Question in the late 1870s, they did it in the spirit of internationalism rather than of nationalism. In the late nineteenth century British nationalism, as we have seen, was largely of the conservative kind. As in France and Germany in the decades before 1914, such nationalism increasingly took the form of imperialism.

If conservative nationalism, largely in the shape of great-power imperialism, culminated in WWI, liberal nationalism came to fruition in the peace treaties of 1919. To the extent that the Versailles settlement rested on the principle of national self-determination and the ideal of constitutional democracy, it might be seen as the realization of what in many European nations had been the central parts of the traditional program of liberal nationalism. The establishment of the League of Nations, however, confirmed the shift of emphasis from the nationalist to the internationalist strand of liberalism that had already taken place, particularly in the English-speaking countries of the world but also in many small countries in Europe. Though representing a compromise between different schools and interests, this institution inaugurated a decade of liberal internationalist dominance in the European thought of most of its members. That period came to an end when, once again, the rise of conservative nationalism, this time in the extremist form of central and south European fascism, sidelined liberal thought in most parts of the Continent.

Modern Appearances

Most of the half century after 1945 liberal nationalism was not a major force in European politics. When it asserted itself, it was usually as a reaction to manifestations of some form or other of internationalism. The most forceful challenge to European liberal feelings in the later 1940s was that of the

Soviet Union in what became known as Eastern Europe. Having left large detachments of troops in those parts of eastern and central Europe that the Red Army had conquered in the later stages of the war, the Russians soon began the process of imposing communist governments in all countries under their control. Whatever local opposition they encountered was, however, only rarely inspired by liberal nationalism. The countries of Eastern Europe, most of which had obtained their independent statehood fairly recently, had strong traditions of political nationalism, which in some cases had gained added strength through anti-German resistance during the war. But, as we have seen, their nationalism was largely of a conservative, sometimes fascist kind. Apart from Czechoslovakia, they had no solid democratic tradition, and no organized liberal parties and movements to match the well-organized and Soviet-supported communists.

In the last years of Stalin and the first years of his successors, in Eastern Europe a period of political suppression, cultural censorship and economic hardship, hybrid forms of anti-Soviet nationalism developed in several people's democracies. Some strands of that nationalism were liberal. The events in Poland and Hungary in 1956 not only marked the emergence of a new form of communist nationalism at the governmental level but also reflected the presence of liberal ideas and feelings among the public. While workers and peasants demonstrated against Poland's subordination to the Soviet Union, writers and students demanded restoration of the cultural independence of the country and renewal of its contacts with the West.[16] In Hungary, a prominent group of young intellectuals called for the readoption of the coat of arms of Kossuth, the patriotic hero of 1848, the restoration of national sovereignty in relations with the Soviet Union and the introduction of legal and social justice for all.[17] But in both countries the developing communist nationalism within the governing parties proved a rather more formative influence on relations with the Soviet Union than the liberal feelings of certain sections of the public and the Western orientations of some parts of the intelligentsia.

In the crises and revolutions of 1989, however, the liberal element in anti-Soviet nationalism came more to the forefront. In most countries, East European nationalism was by then much more than essentially a protest against Soviet domination of the external relations and control of the internal politics of the people's democracies. Often directed also against the policies and practices of the local régime, such nationalism had pronounced anticommunist and significant pro-democratic elements. With the collapse of communist governments came a further shift of emphasis toward the liberal nationalist programs. In Poland, where the alternative trade union movement, Solidarity, had been legalized and allowed to form a channel for anti-soviet and anticommunist sentiments and ideas, roundtable negotiations with the government led to partly free elections. The sweeping victory of Solidarity, which spelt the end of communist rule, presented an opening for a revival of democratic policies and experiments with a market economy as well as for other liberal pursuits. In Hungary, where political liberalization under the communist government had gone further than in the other people's democracies, a relatively smooth transition to democracy prepared the way for the pursuit of traditional liberal goals. In Czechoslovakia, where for some years Charter 77 and other groups of intellectuals, artists and students opposed to Soviet domination and communist government had discreetly canvassed liberal ideas, the collapse of the government in Prague led to the restoration of liberal democracy and the introduction of a market economy in a new Czech Republic under the presidency of Vaclav Havel, the foremost intellectual opponent of the old régime. But, whatever its ideological role and political importance in the events of the late 1980s, liberal nationalism in those countries was in the early 1990s rapidly eclipsed by nonsocialist forms of internationalism, the primary political goals of which were security through the protection of NATO and prosperity through membership of the EC.

On the eve of the disintegration of Yugoslavia and the Soviet Union, liberal nationalism in these countries was directed largely at the territorial structure of the multinational state. However, the breakdown of their highly centralized form of rule, by swiftly removing the principal obstacle to more liberal kinds of government, in principle tended to facilitate the development of secessionist policies with democratic inclinations. But, as in the breakup of the multinational empires of pre-1914 Europe, the goals of the rising nationalities and emerging republics were more in the nature of territorial revision than of political liberalization. Whatever the precise nature and relative influence of liberal nationalism in these countries at this stage of history, it did not thrive for long. Once the secessionist efforts had led to crisis or war with the former government, rivaling nationalities or neighboring republics, it was soon transformed into, or else eclipsed by, aggressive forms of conservative nationalism. Conditioned by war or civil war, the latter nationalism usually became the principal motivating force in the defense of national interests and pursuit of territorial goals.

If liberal nationalism in Eastern Europe was mainly a reaction to communist internationalism, in Western Europe it was usually a defensive response to political expressions and institutional manifestations of various other forms of internationalism, whether conservative, social democratic or even liberal. Opposed to the political, economic or cultural influence of one or both of the superpowers and to the growing importance of European major powers, in particular the Federal Republic of Germany, liberal nationalism was directed mainly against NATO and the European Communities. Though it appeared in mild, and occasionally less mild, forms in most of the Western countries, it was most influential in some of the smaller states.

In relation to NATO, liberal nationalism was opposed to its leadership, in particular the role of the United States, to its policies and programs or even to membership of the alliance. In Denmark, the political party that in the first postwar decades came closest to exhibiting such attitudes was the Radical Liberals. Still guided by pacifist, antimilitarist and neutralist traditions of thought, it was from the outset against Denmark accepting membership of NATO and becoming involved in the rivalry of the superpowers and the growing conflict between East and West in European politics. After the country had become a founding member of NATO, the party focused its criticism on the policies and activities of the alliance, in the 1950s rejecting various forms of military cooperation with the allies and in later decades often exercising a restraining influence on Danish alliance policy.[18] The negative or halfhearted Radical Liberal attitude to NATO was apparently inspired less by conventional nationalism than by Nordic feelings. Nationalism, whether of the liberal or of any other kind, was not a marked feature of Danish politics, at least not in the postwar years and the first decades of the cold war. Its place in the hearts and minds of many people was taken by a firm commitment to Scandinavian cooperation and the Nordic idea, which might be seen as representing a kind of extended nationalism.

A more clear-cut case of liberal nationalist opposition to NATO was presented by Greece in the 1950s and 1960s. As early as 1953, the year after its accession to the treaty, a parliamentary alliance dominated by Centrists and Liberals voted against ratification of an agreement reached between the conservative government of Marshal Papagos and the American administration that gave NATO and the United States extensive military facilities in Greece. The Liberals, together with the Left, argued that the Greek government should have refused commitments of such magnitude. In the mid-1960s, after a series of Greek–Turkish crises over Cyprus, rising political anger with the Western powers and frequent street demonstrations against NATO and the United States, the liberal Center Union government of George Papandreou gave expression to national passions when it reacted to the alliance leader insisting on following an evenhanded course in the conflict between Greece and its archenemy. It cut the defense budget despite strong objections from NATO, imposed restrictions on Greek participation in particular allied exercises and allowed the government-controlled radio and the pro-government press to air anti-American sentiments.[19] After the seven years interregnum of the Colonels, an equally nationalistic policy was adopted by Andreas Papandreou, who again enjoyed the backing of a public hostile to NATO and the United States. The party-political label of the revived nationalism, however, was now social democratic rather than liberal.

Though motivated by quite different political considerations, both the Danish Radical Liberals and the Greek Liberals found themselves in opposition to the organization and policies of collective defense that constituted the principal manifestations of pluralist conservative internationalism. Liberal nationalists who criticized the structure and activities of the European Communities came up against other forms of internationalism. In the earlier years, especially in the 1950s and 1960s, their case was to a considerable extent a reaction to the solidarist conservative internationalism of most of the founders of the first Communities. In later decades it was also a response to the social democratic internationalism of many of the Eurocrats. While the corporatist outlook and *dirigist* tendencies of the former kind of European internationalism offended liberals in most countries, the social orientations and ideological commitment to economic planning and central control of the latter also went against the grain. Even the European engagement of liberal internationalism as manifested in the common market of the EEC and the international organs of the other Communities, the Danish case suggests, could be too much for some liberal nationalists.

Denmark presented a case of diverse Liberal attitudes to the European Communities. The establishment of the ECSC and the signing of the Rome treaty inspired little enthusiasm among either Liberals or Radical Liberals. In common with the other Danish political parties, neither party showed much interest in the corporate integration and federal program of the 1950s and 1960s. Even the debate in the early 1970s, preceding the accession to the EEC in 1973, focused on the economic advantages and disadvantages of joining, and not on the long-term goals of the European federalists. Not till the debate about the Single European Act in 1985 did the notion of a European union come to the forefront. By then the Liberals, led by Uffe Ellemann-Jensen who was foreign minister in a coalition government, had come out strongly in favor of strengthening the organs of the EC, in particular the Parliament, and developing the EPC. As the most pro-European of the Danish political parties, they seemed to be moved mainly by traditional liberal internationalist convictions but to some extent also by Europeanist ideas and sentiments of a sort which, in an extra-European perspective, could be seen as betraying a tendency toward a liberal nationalism writ large and directed at the emerging body of the EC.

The Radical Liberals, however, remained much more skeptical of the federalist tendencies in Western Europe. Insisting on a highly pragmatic and piecemeal approach to the process of integration, they were against a consolidation of the EPC and opposed to the Single European Act, on the grounds that they could not countenance a union that placed formal restrictions on Danish foreign policy.[20] If the Liberal position in that debate reflected a regional internationalism that was supported by a measure of extended nationalism, the Radical Liberal position expressed a narrower and more nationalist attitude. Though Radical Liberal nationalism, too, might be extended to cover a wider geographical area with respect to some matters, it rarely stretched beyond the Nordic region.

Liberal nationalism in the second half of the twentieth century was opposed, in some place or other and at one time or another, to almost any kind of internationalism—to communist internationalism in Eastern Europe and to pluralist conservative, solidarist conservative, social democratic and occasionally even liberal internationalism in Western Europe. But most of the time it was a weaker force in European politics than not only conservative but also socialist nationalism. If current efforts to deepen and widen the EU are maintained, liberal nationalism may well be revived in the next decades of European history.

CHAPTER 6

Socialist Nationalism

V ery much a twentieth-century phenomenon, the third form of nationalism distinguished here is of far more recent origin than both conservative and liberal nationalism. Usually motivated by a concern to protect achievements accomplished or reach goals pursued in national politics, socialist nationalism has at some time or other been directed against every form of internationalism, including some socialist varieties. It has been mainly reactive and defensive.

Three types of socialist nationalism may be distinguished in the European politics of the second half of the twentieth century. While a communist type left its mark on the international relations of Eastern Europe up to the end of the cold war, a social democratic type gained some influence in Western Europe during the early postwar decades. After the détente in East–West relations in the 1960s, West European socialist parties and movements to the left of the social democrats developed a nationalism with some novel features.

Origins and Development

The origins of both communist and social democratic nationalism may be traced to the deeds of socialist parties and the revisions of socialist thought in the later years of the nineteenth and earlier part of the twentieth century. A suitable starting point for outlining the development of communist nationalism may be the eve of WWI, when the socialists in each country had to decide whether to oppose the war or to support their government. Instead of acting upon successive resolutions of the Second International and, in the name of transnational solidarity of the working classes of industrialized nations, refusing to support the war efforts, they started a debate about which kind of war might require their support and how they should offer it. The large German party, as well as socialist parties in other countries involved in the war, decided to back their governments. Thus, they showed that the international solidarity of the working classes was too feeble to overcome the national concerns of each party in a situation of major international crisis. Contrary to the assertions of Marx and Engels, proletarian harmony was eclipsed by interstate conflict. It was not merely that many socialists, like most bourgeois people, were overwhelmed with patriotism in a moment of national emergency. It was also that each party feared that its achievements and opportunities in the cause of socialism might be lost if the country within which it had waged its struggle and was still pursuing its goals were defeated in war. When it came to the point, their orientation was already national rather than transnational.

Lenin, deeply disappointed by socialist reactions to the prospect of major war, rescued the crucial doctrine of proletarian harmony of interests and solidarity in action by highlighting the notion of a revolutionary vanguard and stressing the importance of the leaders. Through strict discipline they would ensure that socialist parties and movements concentrated their efforts on the transnational goal of overthrowing capitalism, rather than on their various national preoccupations. Thus, ideologically, Lenin managed to repair and strengthen the defenses of proletarian internationalism. At the level of political action, however, he played a central part in events that, as they turned out, indirectly helped to facilitate the development of a communist nationalism.

That the Russian Revolution of 1917 did not lead to European revolution, followed by a collapse of the capitalist system, but brought about civil war in Russia and intervention by foreign powers tended to create from the outset a siege mentality in the Bolshevik régime. Deeming the intervention of Russia's former allies as counterrevolutionary, it developed a lasting notion of capitalist encirclement of the Soviet Union. Against this background its leaders revised their conceptions of Soviet relations with the rest of the world and formulated a new policy for their country. Lenin, introducing the notions of uneven development of nations and prolonged existence of state differences, accepted the need for maintaining the proletarian state to deal with neighbors and enemies of the Soviet Union. Stalin, using the slogan of socialism in one country, laid down a policy of intense industrialization and enforced collectivization, which involved a shift of emphasis from international revolution toward internal development. His theorists, building on Leninist revisions of orthodox Marxism, acknowledged the necessity of maintaining the whole apparatus of the state while the Soviet Union was the only country that had taken the road toward socialism. The emphasis on the development of the economy and the acceptance of the prolongation of the life of the state amounted to a compromise between the goals of international socialism and the needs of the Soviet Union.

It was a compromise that allowed Russian national feelings to reassert themselves and play an increasingly important role in the political life of the Soviet Union. Through economic five-year plans, agricultural collectivization and rearmament, Stalin succeeded in making the Soviet Union a great power. Despite the immense suffering involved in carrying out the program of the 1920s and 1930s, the population on the whole identified with the society that was taking shape and backed the power that was emerging on the European scene. The rise of fascism in Europe and the potential threat from Nazi Germany strengthened such support, as did the coming of war. More than anything else, it was the German invasion in June 1941 that revived nationalism in the Soviet Union. In four years of patriotic war, fought under Stalin's leadership, nationalism reached new heights.

At the end of the war, when the Red Army occupied large parts of eastern and central Europe and the Soviet Union enjoyed substantial support in several West European countries, this nationalism was projected onto Europe. Together with communist internationalism, it became an element in the ideology that from the outset of the cold war guided Soviet relations with the new people's democracies of Eastern Europe. Though always presented in terms of socialist or proletarian internationalism, this ideology obviously reflected not only transnational socialist goals but also Soviet national interests. Defined and interpreted in Moscow, it became the theoretical basis for constructing a Socialist Commonwealth as well as for maintaining Soviet control of its constituent members. Drawing on both internationalism and nationalism, it had much in common with nonsocialist forms of great-power imperialism. As we shall see, the socialist nationalism that developed in Eastern Europe was largely a reaction to the self-serving element in the socialist internationalism promulgated by the Soviet Union. The tendency toward a more national orientation that marked the policies of some communist and other leftist parties in Western Europe in the later decades of the cold war, was also partly a response to the Soviet type of internationalism.

If communist nationalism in the Soviet Union, as well as its counterparts in Eastern and Western Europe, may be seen as indirect results of certain events in socialist history and subsequent revisions of socialist thought, social democratic nationalism in the second half of the twentieth century represents a more direct development from earlier socialist thought and action.

At the theoretical level, the principal source of the latter strand of socialist nationalism was the revisions of the ideology of Marx and Engels and other innovations in socialist thought introduced in the last years of the nineteenth and the first decades of the twentieth century. With the shift from rapid transformation of society through revolution to slow evolution through reform came a new attitude to the state. As the parliamentary successes of the German social democrats had shown, the established channels of the state machinery could be useful in the pursuit of socialist goals. By improving the state in their own country, instead of waiting for the situation to arise in which it was supposed to wither, socialists could equip themselves with a tool that might allow them to pursue their policies and achieve some of their ambitions already in the existing situation.

Advocating step-by-step reform of society within each country, rather than dreaming about distant goals and plotting transnational revolution, Edward Bernstein in Germany, Jean Jaurès in France, the Fabians in England and others elsewhere accepted the state as an instrument of social, economic and political progress. In doing so, they and their followers soon came to see the state in much the same terms as many nonsocialist writers and politicians, namely as the embodiment of national unity and thus an object of national feeling. Improving the state, they thought, could be not only a means of furthering specific socialist goals but also a way of generally overcoming the divisions and struggles resulting from the class structure of national society. "Only socialism . . . ," Jaurès predicted, "will resolve the antagonism of classes and make of each nation, finally at peace internally, a particle of humanity."[1] Shaping states in the social democratic image, such writers tended to assume, could also help to reduce international conflict. States resting on social democratic principles would be less aggressive than traditional states, they expected, and hence relations among them more peaceful. If their faith in the possibility of bringing welfare to the people by improving the state prepared the ground for an ideological and emotional attachment to the nation, social democratic national beliefs and feelings, it seemed, would go hand in hand with a social democratic form of internationalism.

The explicit acceptance of the state and implicit commitment to the nationality principle apparent in the revisionist writings of the pre-1914 years were consolidated through the political experience of reformist socialists in the decades between WWI and WWII. In national politics, this was a period in which socialist parties and movements strengthened their parliamentary positions in various parts of Europe, in some countries, notably the Scandinavian ones and Britain, even assuming governmental power. The closer they came to office, the easier they found it to identify with the nation. In international politics, the interwar years were an age of growing conflict between the interests and policies of the major European powers and of rising diplomatic tension in the region. With the establishment of fascism and the decline of the League of Nations in the 1930s it became increasingly difficult to maintain the mild social democratic internationalism of the 1920s. Both national and international circumstances were more conducive to identification with the nation and expression of nationalist sentiments and ideas. With the approach of WWII the leaders and supporters of the Social Democratic and labor parties rallied behind their governments, as they had done in 1914. The resoluteness with which they supported national policy after the outbreak of hostilities, whether it was to help defeat the fascist powers or to stay neutral, seemed to be inspired by nationalism rather than internationalism.

The ideological and political division between reformist and revolutionary socialists was reflected not least in their reactions to military occupation of the countries invaded by Germany in the first years of the war. The social democrats and other reformist socialist parties, whether or not they were in government, in general reacted essentially nationally. Together with nonsocialist parties, they set up exile governments on allied soil or, in the first years, engaged the occupying power in a mixture of reluctant cooperation and passive resistance and, later in the war, took up active resistance. The communists reacted more internationally. Between the signing of the Nazi–Soviet Pact in 1939 and the German invasion of the Soviet Union in 1941 they kept the lowest possible profile, but during the rest of the war they engaged in armed resistance. Though undoubtedly tempered by national feelings, their response to Nazi occupation was basically motivated by internationalist commitment to the pursuit of socialist goals. While the social democrats and others accepted help from the Western allies in the national struggle, the communists took their orders from Moscow in the name of international solidarity.

Communist Type

Paradoxically, some of the most marked expressions of socialist nationalism in the postwar decades occurred not in West European countries with social democratic or labor parties but among the communist countries of Eastern Europe. While other kinds of nationalism had deep domestic roots in most of these countries, its emergence in the communist form was generally more a result of external conditions. The major foreign influence was the policy of the Soviet Union toward countries that had taken the path toward socialism. The mixture of doctrinaire internationalist ideology and brutal national self-interest that guided Soviet conduct of relations with Tito's Yugoslavia and the people's democracies provoked nationalist reactions in most cases. Another influence was the example of the Soviet Union itself. Stalin had already, long before the war, given communism a national face through his pursuit of socialism in one country, and had during the war deliberately invoked the nationalist forces of Russia as well as of several nations in southeastern Europe involved in the struggle of liberation from Nazi occupation. Thus, there were high-level precedents for qualifying official internationalism with some discreet nationalism.

The communist type of nationalism that emerged after the rupture of relations between Moscow and Belgrade and the establishment of people's democracies in the countries liberated by the Red Army was governmental rather than public. Though it often enjoyed some popular support, it was developed and sustained mainly by the leaders of the communist parties and rulers of the states. Invoked largely to protect the sovereign rights of the country and the political interests of the régime, it was essentially defensive. Being typically a reaction to demands from the Soviet leadership, such nationalism often reflected the nature of the pressure exerted by Moscow, sometimes taking a political and at other times an economic form.

The most conspicuous, though ultimately perhaps also the least substantial, case of communist nationalism was that of Tito's Yugoslavia. The year 1948, when the Communist Party of Yugoslavia was expelled from Cominform, became a turning point in the ideological orientation of the new Yugoslavia. The open rupture between Stalin and Tito led to a rapid decline of the communist internationalism that on the whole had prevailed in Yugoslav external relations in the final part of the war and in the immediate postwar period. In its foreign policy during the cold war, Yugoslavia developed a new form of internationalism that found expression in support for the emerging nonaligned movement of the Third World, instead of in loyalty toward the communist bloc directed from Moscow. The rupture of relations with the Soviet Union also brought about a steep rise of a communist kind of Yugoslavism—as it has been called in order to distinguish it from the particularistic nationalisms of the Serbs, Croats and other peoples making up the country. In the arrangement of domestic affairs, Yugoslav economists and ideologists evolved a national version of communism that presented a number of novel and comparatively liberal features, some of them incorporating elements of a market economy. To Soviet leaders and ideologists, Yugoslav nationalism and communism constituted a threat to the cohesion of the bloc and the leadership of the Soviet Union. Rejecting Yugoslav ideas and policies as a deviation from orthodoxy, Stalin's successors condemned them as "revisionism."

In the course of the diplomatic and ideological conflict between the Soviet leaders and Tito and his advisers, which continued during most of the cold war, Yugoslav nationalism grew stronger. Struggling against what he called "big-power chauvinism" and trying to balance between the blocs of the East and the West, Tito sought to promote and consolidate a collective national feeling strong enough to ensure the survival of his country and protect its independence. However, encouraging Yugoslav nationalism was for him more than a defensive measure against the threats and temptations presented by the superpowers. It could also serve domestic and regional purposes. Inspired by the vision of a united Yugoslavia occupying a central role in Balkan politics, he tried to overcome the historical tensions among the Yugoslav peoples by fostering a collective pride in the achievements of their country.

Tito's death in 1980 did not immediately lead to the eclipse of communist nationalism in Yugoslavia. Not till after the end of the cold war did particularistic nationalism obliterate all forms of Yugoslavism. That the state collapsed into war and civil war so soon after the disappearance of the East–West division in European and global politics indicates that communist Yugoslavism was not simply a product of the will power of the leadership of the state but also an effect of the dynamics of dualistic conflict in the states system. If in the interwar period it had been primarily a revisionist encirclement of the new state by Italy, Hungary and Bulgaria that had given Yugoslavia political unity and national consciousness, during the cold war it was basically the polarizing forces of high tension in the international system that conditioned Yugoslav identity and communist nationalism.

At the local level of Balkan politics, the postwar issue with Bulgaria about the future of Macedonia and other matters presented an additional, though less important, external incentive to Yugoslav nationalism. This issue also played a role in the development of Bulgarian nationalism. The recurrent clash of competing nationalisms affected relations between the two countries for much of the cold war, but was usually contained within the ideological framework of international communism. Since Bulgaria was essentially reacting to Tito's endeavors to create a big Macedonia and incorporate it in a Yugoslav–Bulgarian federation under Yugoslav leadership—a policy which initially enjoyed Soviet support—its nationalism was largely defensive.

The defensive character of Bulgarian nationalism was even more apparent in the conduct of relations with the Soviet Union. Traicho Kostov, secretary of the Communist Party in the late 1940s and likely successor of its leader Georgi Dimitrov, is an early example. Before his trial and execution as a Titoist in 1949, he took a nationalist stand in Moscow, complaining in Stalin's presence about injustices in Soviet–Bulgarian agreements.[2] After his exoneration, which followed the accession of Zhivkov, Kostov became a model for those Bulgarians who believed that a communist should put his own country's interests before the principle of international solidarity when dealing with other communist countries. Mainly directed against Soviet control and exploitation of other communist states, the nationalism of Bulgarian communists took political as well as economic forms. In the internal affairs of the country, it also found cultural expression. After the demise of Stalin, the régime felt free to seek to strengthen its hand by reviving and consolidating a wide range of national traditions and institutions.[3]

On the whole, however, the Bulgarian government was careful not to give free rein to its nationalist tendencies. As in most other people's democracies, the leaders of the party knew that it might be unwise to cause too much offence in Moscow, since the survival of the régime in Sofia could ultimately depend on the support of the Soviet Union. Rumania took a different line. The Stalinist and post-Stalinist pressures on the satellites to conform gradually brought about an ideological reorientation in the Rumanian leadership, from the socialist internationalism of the postwar period toward a fairly pronounced nationalism. Determined to maintain the nation's political identity against growing Soviet influence, Georghe Georghiu-Dej and his associates in the mid-1950s upheld and defended the historical tradition of Rumania. Khrushchev's internationalist policy in the following period provoked Bucharest to stress the national legacy even more. Soon some of the elements of conservative nationalism of precommunist years, including anti-Semitism, anti-Hungarian postures and chauvinism, reemerged and became part of a growing communist nationalism.[4]

In the 1960s the nationalism of the Rumanian régime was expressed primarily through its economic policies. When the Soviet leadership, acting through COMECON, tried to impose upon the bloc an economic division of labor based on the current level of development of each of its members, the Rumanian government reacted with nationalist fervor. In March 1963 the Central Committee denounced the proposals and invoked the principles of national sovereignty and equal rights. Even after the scheme was shelved, which was largely a result of the Rumanian veto, the government continued its opposition to Soviet impositions, in particular to further efforts toward full economic integration of the bloc. In its relations with other communist countries it maintained an independence that no other member of the bloc had dared to pursue. Assuming a neutral role in the Sino-Soviet dispute, it established ties with China and Albania and developed economic relations with the West, especially Bonn.

In spearheading communist nationalism, however, the régime was not merely endeavoring to protect the country against political control and economic exploitation by the dominant power in the Socialist Common-wealth. It was also trying to secure public acceptance of the political, economic, social and cultural program of Rumanian communism. The con-cluding part of Nicolae Ceaucesco's address to the Constituent Assembly in August 1965, delivered soon after his accession to power, revealed the nature and role of a nationalism intended to prepare the ground for a national socialist society:

> We are summoned, comrade deputies, to adopt the fundamental law of Socialist Rumania embodying the most daring dreams of our people, the dreams for which our best sons have fought, worked and died. Unlimited opportunities loom on the horizon; no previous generation has been for-tunate enough to participate in such grandiose social changes, to be on the threshold of national glory. What greater wish could anyone have than to take part in the struggle and work for the attainment of his country's glorious future, for the progress and prosperity of his Fatherland.
>
> We are convinced that, under the leadership of the Rumanian Communist Party, the working people will spare no effort to develop the socialist economy and culture, to pave the way for the triumphant march toward the society in which all our people's activities will flourish and in which all who work will lead a life of plenty and happiness—the Communist society.[5]

Though he appealed for public support, Ceaucesco made no concessions to the people in matters of political control and economic direction but ruled his country with a severity reminiscent of Stalin's ways. In this respect, his régime took a different course from that of the Hungarian communist gov-ernment, which also sought domestic popularity through nationalist appeals.

In the late 1940s the Communist Party of Hungary, which the Red Army had imposed on the country, found it hard to maintain its power. In an attempt to secure some public support, it appealed to the patriotic instincts of the masses, at the same time suppressing older, bourgeois forms of nation-alism. Claiming to be the true heir of the ideas of 1848, it stressed the his-torical theme of a struggle for independence and upheld the Magyar national concept. But the régime failed to bring about a national revival. Usually loyal to the Soviet Union in bloc politics, generally ineffective in economic man-agement and always repressive in domestic politics, it was in no position to spearhead a communist form of Hungarian nationalism.

For a brief while the government of Imre Nagy, who enjoyed a reputation as a liberal communist, seemed close to taking on such a role. In the confused situation of October 1956 his independent line in foreign policy, which in negotiations with Moscow involved demands for withdrawal of Soviet troops, release from the Warsaw Pact and even acceptance of neutral status between East and West, drew a considerable measure of public support. Popular patriotism and governmental nationalism seemed to be coming together in joint opposition to Soviet domination. But this situation did not survive the crushing of the Hungarian rebellion by Soviet tanks.

The installation of János Kádár and the imposition of martial law led to "normalization" of the internal and external situation of the country, which involved a suppression of the liberal and nationalist passions of 1956. Subsequently, however, the economic and political condition of the country began to undergo a gradual liberalization. Staying in power for thirty-two years, Kádár saw his way to introduce economic reforms, soften political repression and open up contacts with Western countries, and still maintain relatively good terms with the Soviet Union. Under his leadership, Hungary became politically and socially stable. But it was a stability that rested on political apathy rather than on public identification with the régime. With little ideological debate, the later decades of Hungarian communism became a period of political pragmatism. If the régime before 1956 had assumed a nationalist pose without allowing liberal reform, the government of Kádár introduced liberalizing measures without encouraging nationalist tendencies. The later months of 1956, when Hungarian communism was exposed to nationalist and liberalizing influences at the same time, were an exceptional period.

Poland presented a rather more substantial example of communist nationalism. In that country, too, 1956 marked the high point of nationalist influences on the ideas and policies of the régime. At the popular level, however, nationalist sentiments were already intense and widespread in the earlier postwar years. They were expressed primarily in a strong hatred of the Germans, which was rooted in earlier periods of history and nourished by recent memories of wartime atrocities. But such sentiments were directed against the Russians too, partly because of wartime experience of Soviet rule but mainly as a result of heavy-handed Soviet interference in Polish politics in the late 1940s. The newly emergent communist régime made a point of drawing on those anti-German feelings in order to secure some support for its pro-Soviet policies. In a situation of widespread concern about the safety of recently acquired and formerly German territories and growing anxiety about the prospect of German rearmament, it succeeded in harnessing some of the nationalist fears and animosities to the policy of accepting the lesser evil of Soviet control and interference. Thus the communist ideology of the postwar period incorporated certain elements of Polish nationalism.

It was not till 1956, when Stalinism was losing its grip in the Soviet Union and some of its satellites and voicing dissatisfaction with Soviet domination was becoming slightly less dangerous, that communist nationalism in Poland became targeted at the Soviet Union. At that stage, nationalist tendencies were widespread within the ruling party itself. Various developments in the political life of the country since the war, and of the bloc since 1948, had led to the emergence of a form of national communism, which eventually displayed characteristics at odds with Soviet-led internationalism. One such development had been the communist practice of appealing to the patriotic feelings and exploiting the nationalist sentiments of the public when seeking to gain support for policies and broaden the membership of the party. Started during the war and continued after its end, this habit had attracted many new members with nationalist convictions and had left its mark on the ideological orientation of the party. So had the fusion in 1948 of the Socialists with the Polish Workers' Party, the renamed Communist Party. The Socialists had brought with them some of the elements of prewar nationalism. A third influence had been the example of Yugoslavia. Tito had demonstrated that it was practicable for a communist state to pursue independent policies in both domestic affairs and external relations and that it was possible to combine the ideologies of nationalism and communism. More than any other influence, it was the Yugoslav model that now helped to turn the nationalist tendencies in the party against the Soviet Union.[6]

At the popular level, 1956 was the year of a nationalist upsurge that was directed primarily against the Soviet Union. Reacting to years of political domination, economic exploitation and cultural impositions by Moscow, workers, intellectuals and students demonstrated against the subordination of their nation and demanded independence in all spheres. For a while the régime, now under the leadership of Wladyslaw Gomulka who until 1954 had been imprisoned as a "national deviationist," spearheaded the popular movement by championing the cause of national communism. The initial results of the events of "October" were greater internal and external freedom for the country, within the framework of the Soviet bloc, and acceptance of the concept of "a Polish way to socialism aiming at the consolidation of socialist democracy and Polish sovereignty."[7] But soon the anti-soviet tendencies of 1956, both within the party and in the populace, were firmly restrained. Before long communist nationalism in Poland again rested mainly on anti-German sentiments, and periodically on anti-Semitism as well.

Moreover, the Gomulka régime gradually reversed many of the liberal and progressive gains of October, with the result that Poland within a decade of 1956 became one of the most orthodox of the people's democracies.

The intellectual excitement and political engagement that had characterized the mid-1950s were followed by a long period of cynicism and apathy. During the 1960s and 1970s it became increasingly clear that only few Poles, whether within the ranks of the party or in the country at large, had faith in the communist cause.

At the beginning of the 1980s, before the military rule of Wojciech Jaruzelski, the two most influential popular movements in the country were the newly established Solidarity, which represented a coalition of opposition forces, and the Roman Catholic Church, which most of the time had been hostile to the communist movement. If, at that stage, the stronger political challenge to entrenched communism came from Solidarity, the real ideological opposition was still the Catholic Church, which stood for a belief system that, like contemporary communism itself, had both internationalist and nationalist elements. While communism, in its internationalist as well as its nationalist aspect, had lost its ideological appeal, Catholicism as an anticommunist religion had retained its influence upon the minds of the people. An early casualty in the ideological conflict had been communist nationalism, which in the years after 1956 had been outshone by the basically conservative nationalism of the Church.

In Czechoslovakia, there was little anti-soviet communist nationalism. In the decades before the "Prague spring" of 1968 as well as in the period up to the revolution in 1989, this country was nearly always a model satellite. The Communist Party enjoyed wide popular support when it seized power in 1948, and thus started its rule in circumstances very different from those obtaining in Hungary and Poland. Later, after years of repression by Stalinist methods, the population turned politically docile. Even the exciting events of 1968 failed to bring forth strong anti-soviet sentiments. The liberalists of the brief Dubcek period wanted more democracy within the party and more trade with the West, but were not firmly against Soviet leadership of the bloc or Czechoslovak membership of the WTO and the CMEA. After 1968, extensive purges and brutal repression once again reduced the people to a state of political apathy.

Most of the communist nationalism that did manifest itself in the political life of Czechoslovakia was directed not against external forces and influences but against the internal structure and processes of the state itself. The challenge came from the Slovak Communist Party, which constantly expressed widespread national dissatisfaction with a centralist constitution that gave Slovakia regional autonomy only in form and left ultimate control in the hands of a Czech-dominated régime in Prague. The final result of this issue was the breakup of Czechoslovakia and the emergence of Slovakia as a separate state only a few years after 1989.

In the German Democratic Republic, too, there was only little anti-soviet communist nationalism. At the intergovernmental level, both political needs and strategic considerations stood in the way of such nationalism. East Germany could not do without Soviet support, partly because of the unpopularity of its régime and partly because of its inferiority to West Germany. And the Soviet Union needed the loyalty of East Germany, which was the western outpost of its sphere of influence and hence a strategic pillar of its system of security. Thus, the German Democratic Republic became and remained the most orthodox of the Soviet Union's satellites.

For the subjects of the German Democratic Republic, difficulties of legitimacy and problems of identity impeded patriotic feelings and nationalist passions for their state. A government that, no matter its projection of socialist ideals and cult of the state, relied on repression, depended on Soviet forces stationed on German soil and, not least, represented only the lesser part of Germany could not inspire much national loyalty. Most East Germans, regarding the division of Germany as an accident of history that could not last, focused their national feelings on the entire German community and looked toward some form of reunification.

In the first period of the existence of the East German state the government of Walter Ulbricht, having at the outset declared the creation of a full German nation-state to be among its permanent goals, did not oppose such national feelings among its subjects. But once the Soviet government, after the Federal Republic had joined NATO, had announced that the "German question" had been solved through the setting-up of two German states with different sociopolitical systems, the government rejected the goal of reunification in foreseeable circumstances. In the 1970s, the government of Erich Honecker projected the German Democratic Republic as "a socialist nation" within "a socialist German state," thus by implication denying the existence of a wider German community that included a nonsocialist West Germany. But, though the country by then could boast the highest living standard in COMECON, the government still found it difficult to inculcate a feeling of separate national identity in its subjects. To most people, still inclined to see the division of Germany as a temporary phenomenon, the idea of a separate socialist nation seemed an artificial concept.

Just how insubstantial any national attachment to the German Democratic Republic was became clear the moment the Berlin Wall collapsed. Almost immediately the movement toward unification became unstoppable. As in Czechoslovakia, any nationalism that did exist in East Germany was largely an internal matter, in the sense that it was directed against the legal structure and political processes of Germany. Once the restraints imposed by the cold war had disappeared, such nationalism led rapidly, in one case, to a division of the state into two and, in the other, to a unification of two states.

Though usually governmental and largely defensive, communist nationalism in Eastern Europe differed so much in motivation, nature, form, duration and significance that it defies generalization. Even when developed and expressed by party leaders and government spokesmen, it was often reinforced by public sentiment. Though strictly defensive when aimed at the Soviet Union, it was not always so when directed against smaller neighbors or national minorities. While communist nationalism as a reaction to pressures from abroad was a factor in the external relations of the states, it often served domestic political purposes as well. Though nearly always expressed in political terms, it was often motivated more by economic considerations. At some time or in some countries it was associated with liberalist political, economic and cultural programs or forces, while at other times or in other countries it was linked with repression and stagnation. In some cases it was shortlived, but in others practically a permanent feature. All in all, however, communist nationalism was significant enough to establish both the concept and the fact of national communism. In doing so, it introduced qualifications to orthodox socialist or proletarian internationalism, and set limits to Soviet hegemony in the Socialist Commonwealth.

Nongovernmental manifestations of communist nationalism may be found in the history of West European communist parties. When such parties, in the earlier stages of the cold war, occasionally revealed nationalist tendencies in their policies or appealed to patriotic sentiments in their propaganda, the target of their campaign was usually NATO, the United States, the EEC, international capitalism or some other ideological enemy in the West. From the 1960s, however, most of the parties became more inclined to critically examine the policies and conduct of the Soviet Union as well. While the revelations about Stalin and the crushing of the Hungarian revolution had tested the loyalties of all the parties, the invasion of Czechoslovakia in 1968 gave further pause to both their leaders and their supporters. Some left their party in protest and formed a new political party of their own, while others grew more determined to question the role of the Soviet Union, whether in the international relations of Eastern Europe or in the communist movement as a whole. The result was a gradual estrangement between Moscow and the communist parties in the West.

Moscow's response was to organize a series of conferences, some at world level and others limited to Europe, with a view to revitalizing the Soviet-inspired concept of proletarian internationalism. But the Russians did not succeed in imposing ideological unity and reestablishing political control.

Instead of issuing communiqués expressing solidarity with crucial aspects of Soviet policy, the conferences passed resolutions that stressed the principles of equality and independence of all communist parties and affirmed the legitimacy of interparty criticism.[8] This only served to highlight the growing diversity within the movement and encourage autonomous tendencies in each party. The result was a considerable broadening of the scope for those nationalist tendencies that in the 1960s and 1970s emerged in the political thought of many West European communist parties.

The big Italian Communist Party was the first to acknowledge the pluralist character of Western society and stress the need to allow for specific national features in the formulation of policy. Subsequently other parties elsewhere, both large and smaller ones, pressed for a looser association of parties and less control from the center. Often, a major motivating force was the new nationalism that was gaining influence on the left of the political spectrum. While French communism acquired a novel patriotic appeal that reflected nationalist influences within the party, communism in some small countries, including Holland and most of the Nordic countries, developed noticeable nationalist characteristics. Though labeled with the fashionable prefix Euro, the reformed communism of Western Europe was not uniform but presented a considerable variety of national characteristics.[9]

Although the nationalist tendencies of the different versions of national communism in Western Europe were still directed primarily against NATO, the EC and other manifestations of conservative and liberal internationalism, their major ideological and political significance was to qualify the established doctrines of communist internationalism and check the customary style of leadership of the whole movement. Thus, the reformed communism of West European parties went hand in hand with the national communism in the people's democracies, in the sense that both set limits to socialist internationalism as defined and practiced by the Soviet Union.

Social Democratic Type

While socialist nationalism in the communist camp was in effect opposed to the communist version of socialist internationalism, socialist nationalism in the rest of Europe was largely a reaction to conservative and liberal internationalism. Its principal targets were the leadership and policies of NATO and the goals and programs of the EC. As an offshoot of the reformist tradition of European socialism, it may be described as social democratic nationalism. Generally reflecting the parliamentary fortunes of the social democratic and labor parties, it appeared in both governmental and nongovernmental forms. In some countries it was more pronounced in the first postwar decades, when the North Atlantic alliance and the various European organs were being established, than in later times, when many social democrats and other reformist socialists were more willing to defend their interests and pursue their goals through international cooperation in regional organization.

In some of the larger countries, especially Britain and the Federal Republic of Germany, that kind of nationalism was directed mainly against the integrationist efforts and supranational tendencies prevalent among the core countries of Western Europe. On the occasion of the publication of the Schuman Plan in 1950, Clement Atlee stated that his government could not "accept the principle that the most vital economic forces of this country should be handed over to an authority that is utterly undemocratic and is responsible to nobody."[10] In a report prepared about the same time on the idea of European unity, the international committee of the National Executive of the Labor Party declared that, "in every respect except distance we in Britain are closer to our kinsmen in Australia and New Zealand on the far side of the world than we are to Europe. We are closer in language and in origins, in social habits and institutions, in political outlook and economic interest."[11] A dozen years later Hugh Gaitskell argued that Britain's entry into the EEC would mean the end of a thousand years of British history and would reduce the country to the status of Texas and California.[12] Over the next few decades the balance of power within the Labor movement shifted away from those who were against joining the EEC, mainly the politically influential trade unions and the left wing of the party, toward those with a more European orientation. But the issue between the more nationalist and the more Europeanist sections of the party continued to divide Labor, also after British accession in 1973.

In the Federal Republic, too, most of the social democratic leaders were against the Schuman Plan. Kurt Schumacher, the leader of the party, attacked the plan under the slogan of "the four Ks"—*Kapitalismus, Klerikalismus, Konservatismus, Kartelle*.[13] Whenever they found themselves opposed to the Catholic parties on some issue, the social democrats reacted by denouncing the Europe of the Catholics, predicting that it would be controlled by the Vatican and become reactionary.[14] Though a few of the leaders, notably Willy Brandt, and the unions were Europeanist, the Social Democratic Party was largely nationalist at that stage. Not carrying the nationalist stigma attached to most other parties in postwar Germany, it could afford to appeal openly to national sentiment in the country. The anti-European nationalism of the social democrats was directed mainly against solidarist conservative internationalism, as expounded by some of the founders of the early European Communities. While for the British Labor Party the preferred alternative to European unity was adherence to the British Commonwealth, for the German social democrats it was unification of the two Germanies. In the course of the 1950s and early 1960s, however, the leaders of the SPD came to realize that national unification was not possible in the existing international situation and should not be pursued as an alternative to European integration. Moving toward a decidedly pro-European position, they gradually curbed the nationalist tendencies of the party.

The French and Italian socialists, too, were deeply divided on the European issue for a number of years. While some of them, especially the intellectuals, were bitterly opposed to the efforts at European integration, many others were habitually inclined to pursue their political goals within the national framework. However, though nationalism undoubtedly had some influence in both of those groups, some of the smaller countries provided better examples of social democratic nationalism at work. In Denmark, Norway and Greece, all members of NATO, as well as in nonaligned Sweden, such nationalism was often turned against both the European Communities and the military alliance.

Leftist nationalism was not a factor in Danish politics in the postwar period. The Nordic identification formed in the late 1940s and the Western orientation established after 1949 eclipsed all nationalist sentiments and ideas. Not till the 1960s did the political situation become conducive to a revival of nationalism. The emerging détente in East–West relations, the approaching completion of the first twenty-years period of the North Atlantic alliance and, above all, the prospect of membership of the EC made Danish participation in various forms of Western cooperation once again a matter of public debate. Among those on the left and left of center who objected to some of the policies and activities of NATO or rejected the structure and goals of the EC a new type of nationalism emerged. Though more widespread among the members and supporters of the Socialist People's Party, that nationalism influenced also the large SDP, in particular its Left section. It affected the attitudes and policies of the party primarily by animating latent neutralist inclinations in matters of security and reinforcing an innate reluctance to support federalist drives in Western Europe.

When the social democratic leaders in 1949 decided to depart from the tradition of neutrality and join NATO, many of the members and supporters of the party found it difficult to take sides in the East–West conflict and rearm for collective defense. In subsequent years they were also less than enthusiastic about some of the measures of military preparation that membership of the alliance entailed. Over the years, the neutralist and anti-militarist instincts of the broader sections of the party recaptured some of their traditional influence on its leadership. In the course of the 1960s a new generation of leaders developed a more skeptical view of NATO, eventually coming to see Danish membership of the alliance more as a necessary evil. The tendency for the security policy of the party to move a little closer to the prewar social democratic line was continued in the 1970s under the leadership of Anker Jørgensen. In the 1980s, when the party went into opposition, its new orientation became more conspicuous. On a number of military and strategic issues, relating to the deployment of certain weapons and other matters of some importance for the defense of the region, it opposed agreed policies and qualified established practices of the alliance. In doing so, the leaders enjoyed strong support not only from the left but also from the center of the party as well as from its youth organizations and many sections of the trade unions. Their criticism of the leadership, skepticism about the policies and opposition to the practices of the alliance, complemented by an ingrained optimism about the prospect of reaching agreement with the Russians and securing détente, rested mainly on the traditional ideological bases of neutralism, antimilitarism and pacifism. But sometimes it was apparently also inspired by a new nationalism, according to which Danish interests and values would be better suited by a more minimal role in the alliance.[15]

Social democratic nationalism was perhaps a rather more pronounced feature of the party's attitude to the integrationist movement in Western Europe. Having joined the EC largely for economic reasons, Denmark developed a Community policy in the 1970s and 1980s that, rather like its alliance policy, was characterized by qualified commitment and limited participation. Not till the mid-1980s did the federalist goals of the institution become a subject of serious debate in Danish politics. The occasion was the referendum on the Single European Act. In a fairly heated public debate, which focused on the concept of European union, many social democrats expressed fears that the proposed measures might undermine the powers of the Danish parliament and government. They were particularly concerned about certain tendencies to strengthen the influence of the European parliament, which they found unacceptable. After some internal discussion, the party advised its supporters to vote against the package of proposals. In the following years the party adhered to a highly pragmatic policy of piecemeal integration. In common with other opposition parties, especially the Socialist People's Party, the social democrats again seemed to be motivated partly by nationalist sentiments.[16]

The nationalist tendencies of Danish social democrats, as directed against NATO and the EC, were essentially reactive and defensive. In alliance policy, they were a reaction to the risks associated with being involved in the rivalry of the superpowers and to the requirements arising from membership of the alliance. In Community policy, they were a response to the growing demands and rising expectations associated with the ongoing process of economic and political integration. In both spheres, such tendencies reflected a concern for the sovereign rights and national interests of Denmark and the traditional values of its people, as perceived by members and supporters of the party. After the decline in East–West tension, the revolutions in Eastern Europe, the breaching of the Berlin Wall and, not least, the unification of Germany, the geopolitical situation of Denmark changed so radically that Danish national interests came to appear in a rather different light. In the course of a few months in 1989–90 the social democratic attitude to NATO and the EC changed from a more or less halfhearted commitment to much more willing support, a development that might be seen as reflecting a shift from nationalist reservations toward internationalist engagement.[17]

The influence of socialist nationalism seemed rather more marked in the attitudes and policies of the Norwegian Labor Party, always one of the most radical social democratic parties in northern Europe. The ideological basis of its nationalist tendencies was established in 1921, when the party broke away from the Soviet-sponsored Third International and adopted a strategy of socialism in one country. These tendencies grew more pronounced in the second half of the century, after Norway joined NATO and membership of the EC became a major issue in Norwegian politics. After the mid-1960s they were facilitated by the discovery of rich oil and gas deposits and the expansion of the economic zones off the coasts of the country. As in Denmark, social democratic nationalism was backed more by the Left than by the rest of the party, and was directed against NATO and, in particular, the EC.

In relation to NATO, such nationalism found expression in much the same way as in Denmark, again taking the forms of qualified commitment to the policies and restricted participation in the practices of the alliance. Since practically all the qualifications and restrictions were laid down when the Labor Party was in government, they may reasonably be attributed to that party in particular and seen as reflecting social democratic attitudes more than anything else. The rank and file of the party and, after the decline of the Atlanticists of the postwar period, also many of its leaders were inclined to regard membership of NATO as a necessary evil. Motivated by traditional socialist hostility toward capitalism, imperialism and militarism, they often focused their criticisms on the American leadership of the alliance. To keep Norwegian participation in international power politics to a minimum, they believed, was in the national interest of their country.[18]

The nationalism inherent in the determination to put national concerns before international solidarity was expressed more forcefully in the Labor Party's reactions to the EC and other European institutions. In the earlier debate about joining the EC, which started in the late 1950s and went on till the early 1970s, the left wing of the party was firmly opposed to membership. Rejecting the ultimate goal of a European union and the current tendencies toward supranational decision-making, the opponents took an increasingly nationalist line in their campaign. In the argument preceding the national referendum on membership in 1972 they strengthened their position within the party and, together with anti-marketeers in other parties, secured decisive influence in the referendum, which resulted in a rejection of the invitation to join the EC. In the following decades the left wing of the Labor Party, together with the Socialist Left Party and some members of other parties and movements, maintained a markedly nationalist opposition to the EC, with the result that the referendum in 1994 produced another rejection of membership.

The nationalism of the Labor opponents of the EC was largely of an economic nature. It reached a high point in the 1970s, when it rested on the affluence that oil, gas and fish had given the country, and became prominent again in the debate of the 1990s, when protection of the fishery and agricultural interests of the nation became a central concern. But it had a political dimension as well. The word "union," so prominent in the policy statements of the EC, disturbed many members and supporters of the Labor Party. Evoking the long periods of Norwegian history when the country was ruled from Copenhagen or Stockholm, it connoted authority imposed by a distant and alien government.[19]

In both its economic and political versions, such nationalism was decidedly defensive. Like the nationalism directed against NATO, it was called forth in response to risks and dangers from abroad, whether real or imagined, and expressed in defense of Norwegian rights, interests and values, as perceived by influential sections of the party. After the geopolitical transformation of northern Europe following the end of the cold war and the collapse of the Soviet Union, which made the more farsighted leaders of the party nervous about the prospect of their country becoming marginalized and isolated in foreign policy, nationalist skepticism about NATO declined considerably. But anti-EU nationalism, still governed mainly by economic considerations, remained a major influence on the ideological orientation of the Labor Party, even after Sweden and Finland had joined Denmark in the EU.

Social democratic nationalism in Greece was not always so defensive as in the two Nordic countries. Not primarily a reaction to the policies of NATO and the program of the EC but more a concomitant of local conflict, it was sometimes decidedly aggressive. Like other kinds of Greek nationalism, it was in part an inevitable effect and in part a contributory cause of tense relations with a potential enemy, usually Turkey but in the 1990s also the former Yugoslav republic that seceded from the federation and set itself up as an independent state under the name of Macedonia. Such nationalism was very much associated with the Panhellenic Socialist Movement (PASOK), which under the leadership of Andreas Papandreou established itself as a political party after the fall of the Papadopoulos régime. Three stages may be distinguished in the development of PASOK nationalism.

The first stage lasted from 1974, when Karamanlis returned to power after the demise of the colonels, to 1981, when PASOK won the election and formed its first government. It was a period of radical nationalism, which in its anti-Western aspect was marked initially by passionate denunciation of NATO, the American administration and the Western powers and later by demands for dissociation from both NATO and the EC. In voicing such criticism and making such demands, the party expressed a widely shared public anger with NATO and the Americans for the passive role the allies had played in relation to, first, the coup of 1967 and the rule of the junta and then the Turkish invasion and occupation of part of Cyprus. In its political program, it also responded to the neutralist inclinations then shared by a large part of the population. More broadly, the early nationalism of PASOK, with its strident emphasis on the concept of national sovereignty, reflected the obsession of the Left with the notion of dependence on the West as well as the sensitivity of most Greeks about the place and role of their country in the world.

The second stage lasted from PASOK's accession to power to the disintegration of Yugoslavia. It was distinguished by rather more restraint in the expression of nationalist sentiments and characterized by some willingness to come to terms with both the EC and NATO. One result was that relations with the EC soon became rather different from what had been foreshadowed in past rhetoric. Once they had accepted Greek membership of the Community, the PASOK governments concentrated their efforts on exploiting the economic and financial advantages it offered to the country and the party. Relations with NATO, too, took a new turn. The oft-repeated threats to close the US bases on Greek soil were followed by lengthy negotiations with the Americans and eventual agreement about their military installations. Papandreou hailed the result as a triumph of Greek "national dignity," comparing it with the "colonial" terms endured in the past, and went on to demonstrate Greek independence of the alliance leader in various other ways. The enduring anti-Americanism of the party and its supporters reflected a conviction that the United States was favoring Turkey in the allocation of arms and not supporting Greece diplomatically in the recurrent crises between the two allies. While the mild nationalist tendencies in the alliance policies of the Nordic social democrats were motivated mainly by anxiety not to provoke the Soviet Union and become involved in the regional rivalry of the superpowers, the pronounced anti-American nationalism of the Greek socialists was actuated by frustrated eagerness to secure the support of the United States and NATO in the local conflict with Turkey.[20]

The third stage, which started in the early 1990s, presented a rapid and marked accentuation of the nationalist passions of PASOK. The combination of tense relations with Turkey, collapse of the Yugoslav federation, emergence of a new state with a challenging name on the northern border and general eruption of nationalist rivalry and violence in the Balkans provided a regional environment in which Greek nationalist emotions, socialist as well as conservative, had a much freer rein than in the 1980s. Competing for public support in a domestic situation of nationalist excitement, the leaders of PASOK inveighed against both Turkey and FYROM (the Former Yugoslav Republic of Macedonia) as well as against those outside the Balkans who either failed to support Greece or appeared to side with its potential enemies. The reactions of the European partners, who found Greece intransigent in its hostility toward the republic of Macedonia and disloyal in its tentative support of Serbia, reinforced the Greek sense of alienation from Western Europe and exacerbated the nationalism of PASOK.[21] Whether the negotiated settlement between the warring parties in the former Yugoslavia, the retirement and death of Andreas Papandreou and other regional and national developments brought an end to that stage of PASOK nationalism is not yet clear. The solid anti-Western reactions of the Greek population to the Kosovo intervention indicated that nationalist emotions were still running high among the members and supporters of the party. On the other hand, the style and policies of Constantine Simitis, the new prime minister, suggested that the leadership of the party was now more determined to restrain and control such passions.

The three phases of Greek social democratic nationalism reflected, on one side, the changing external and internal political situation of the country and, on the other side, the developing socialist ideology and populist style of the leadership of the party. But there was another dimension of some importance. The nationalism of PASOK belonged in the context of an East–West dichotomy that for centuries had marked the cultural history of modern Greece. As an expression of Greek populist sentiments, it was rooted in the Eastern heritage and traditions of Byzantium and Orthodoxy; and as a rebellion against habitual dependence on Western power and prestige, it was opposed to the West European influences deriving from the Renaissance and the Enlightenment. The nationalist tendencies of the Greek communists, too, were rooted in the Eastern tradition and opposed to the Western influences in Greek history. But the internationalist framework in which social democratic nationalism was presented was different from that of communist nationalism. When Papandreou, in his appeals to popular sentiments, challenged the economic and political dominance of the West, his frame of reference was the Third World, whereas for the communists of the KKE Party it was the world of the Soviet Union and its allies. In his conduct of relations with countries and people in the Third World, he sometimes went out of his way to cultivate the leaders of some of the more disruptive elements of international society, such as the PLO and Libya. Defying the West in this manner was one of Papandreou's ways of demonstrating the independence of Greece.

In defying a superpower, objecting to East–West polarization and associating with the Third World, Papandreou had something in common with an otherwise quite different Balkan leader, Marshal Tito. Yet, for all his criticism of aspects of capitalism, denunciation of Western powers and institutions and invocation of internationalist concepts of the Third World, Papandreou never took Greece into the nonaligned camp. Though he occasionally, especially in the post-junta period, played upon the neutralist inclinations of some of his supporters, he was not in a position to steer a neutral course in the central conflict of the cold war. Whatever the cultural roots of the Greek people, Papandreou knew that politically and diplomatically Greece belonged with the West.

The best example of neutralist social democratic nationalism may be found in the political history of Sweden in the cold war. From the beginning to the end of the East–West division, Swedish policy was to steer clear of all alignments in order to be able to stay neutral in any crisis or war that might occur between the two sides. Since neutrality had served the country well in both world wars and nonalignment suited its geopolitical situation next to Finland and by the Baltic Sea, it was a policy that enjoyed solid parliamentary and broad popular support. But it was associated with the large Social

Democratic Party in particular. Having governed the country from 1932, seen it through the abortive Scandinavian defense talks in 1948–9 and, except for half a dozen years in the late 1970s and early 1980s, stayed in office throughout the cold war, this party was more responsible than any other for Sweden's policy of keeping out of the East–West conflict.

The social democratic commitment to nonalignment and neutrality was informed with some nationalist feelings. Such sentiments may be detected in the rather parochial and isolationist qualities that marked not only the security policy of the country but also its relations with the EC, notwithstanding the internationalist character of most other areas of its foreign policy. In recurrent debates about affiliation with the Common Market, the stumbling block was not so much the programs of economic integration, which were often recognized as being in Swedish interest, as the goal of political integration, which was generally regarded as irreconcilable with the isolationist doctrine of security policy. Nationalist influence marked even the social democratic attitude to Nordic cooperation, which for most was the preferred alternative to European involvement. On the emotional level, the party was strongly committed to Nordic efforts and solutions, whether in a spirit of local internationalism or of extended nationalism. In practice, however, the party's willingness to engage in Nordic cooperation and integration was often qualified by a rather narrow concern with Swedish national interest.[22]

Even the internationalist side of Swedish foreign policy was somewhat tainted by social democratic nationalism. The government's calls for disarmament, proffering of good offices and involvement in peacekeeping as well as its engagement in the North–South dialogue, support for Third World development and grants of foreign aid occasionally seemed to be imbued with a belief in the moral superiority of a policy of nonalignment and neutrality. Another source of national pride was the economic and social organization of the country. The Swedish model of the welfare state, with its rationalist assumptions, egalitarian principles and tenacious faith in administrative control, was an achievement for which the social democrats could take most of the credit. Collective self-assurance as regards both external relations and domestic arrangements reached its highest point under Olof Palme, who led the party from 1969 till his murder in 1986. Radicalizing the party at home, he assumed the role of spokesman for the conscience of the world and denounced unjust war and tyrannical government anywhere. The moral attitudes and benevolent policies of Sweden in the cold war showed that a nationalist disposition could go hand in hand with internationalist commitment, in a territorially satisfied, economically developed and politically mature small state.

While communist nationalism, as a qualification to the authorized form of communist internationalism, checked the Soviet Union's domination of the Socialist Commonwealth and control of the communist movement, social democratic nationalism, as largely a reaction to conservative and liberal internationalism, limited the efforts of NATO and restrained the ambitions of the EC. The negative implications of the latter nationalism for the effectiveness of the alliance were obvious. Social democratic criticism of the leadership, opposition to particular policies and nonparticipation in various activities of NATO tended to weaken the solidarity of the alliance.

In relation to the conduct and intensity of the superpower rivalry, however, social democratic nationalism had perhaps some beneficial effects. Often motivated, at least in part, by a concern not to provoke the Soviet Union and its allies, it possibly helped to restrain the United States and other major allies in particular situations, thus perhaps occasionally playing a moderating role in tension between the opposed alliances. To the extent that such nationalism was guided, implicitly or explicitly, by neutralist inclinations or convictions, it was bound to have some bearing on the East–West polarization. But nationalist divergence from alliance policy was most often in evidence when tension between the two sides was already low or falling. This suggests that such manifestations of social democratic nationalism were a result as much as a cause of a softening polarization.[23]

The influence of such nationalism on the development of the EC, too, was ambivalent. On the one hand, social democratic opposition to its various supranational tendencies and more ambitious goals tended to slow down the developing process of integration and undermine the long-term program of the institution. On the other hand, to the extent that social democratic nationalism expressed itself in policies that favored a widening of the membership of the Community rather than a deepening of the economic and political integration, it helped to broaden the geographical base and reduce the narrow exclusivity of the central process in European politics. In any case, the social democratic defense of national priorities was an important contribution to that continuing debate about ends and means through which the new Europe is taking shape.

Socialist Type

The third type of socialist nationalism discernible in modern European politics may be dealt with more briefly. It was peculiar to certain opposition parties and popular movements in Western Europe, and usually had only an indirect influence. The large majority of the members and supporters of these parties and movements were socialists and radicals who, on most issues, were to the left of the social democrats, without being communists. The nationalism that they sometimes expressed may be seen as an intermediate variety, somewhere between the communist and the social democratic varieties, within the broad class considered here. Usually tied up with socialist principles and leftist aversions, it may be described by the generic term of socialist nationalism.

In some ways socialist nationalism, in this narrower sense of the term, was more radical than both the communist and the social democratic types. Ideologically, it was generally opposed to all forms of internationalism, except the vague kind of leftist grassroots internationalism entertained by many of its own exponents. It was especially against the conservative internationalism of intergovernmental cooperation, manifested preeminently by NATO, and the liberal internationalism of commercial, financial and institutional bonds, expressed primarily by the EC. Politically, it was in principle against the East as well as the West, being directed in particular at the two superpower rivals, whose nuclear arms race and balance of terror posed the greatest threat to the peoples of Europe. In practice, however, it was targeted especially at the United States and NATO. In Europe, the main target was the EC, which was presented as an emerging capitalist and imperialist superstate. Compared with most social democratic nationalism, socialist nationalism was often expressed more explicitly and aggressively.

The elements of this kind of thought were partly of a traditional socialist and partly of a novel radical kind. Anticapitalism and antimilitarism were basic ingredients and pacifism and neutralism typical components. To these were added a keen concern about the impact of the industrialized world on the physical environment. Hostility toward the economic order of the West and anxiety about the strategic division of the world, in both of which the United States played a leading part, often found expression in a fervent anti-Americanism. While the United States generally evoked repugnance, the Third World sometimes exercised a certain attraction for such socialists. Apt to regard countries of that part of the world as actual or potential victims of superpower rivalry, capitalist exploitation and ecological damage, they were inclined to see them as latent allies or supporters in the struggle with the great powers, multilateral companies and other centers of Western influence. In the view of some socialists—often people who at an earlier stage had looked toward the communist countries for inspiration and guidance—certain countries in the Third World might also present interesting alternative models of economic structure and social order.

Socialist nationalism established itself in Western Europe in the 1960s. The decline in the appeal of Soviet communism in the later part of the previous decade had left many people on the left of the political spectrum with a need for a new set of opinions and principles to guide them. The détente in East–West relations in the early and mid-1960s, which tended to soften the polarization of Europe and widen the scope for national divergence, brought about conditions conducive to a revival of nationalism. The strengthening of NATO and the consolidation of the EEC and other agencies of European integration during the same decade presented palpable targets for leftist nationalism. The student uprisings and social upheavals of 1967–8 animated those who wanted to challenge the entrenched authorities and upset the existing systems. Conditioned, challenged and stimulated by international and national developments in the 1960s, socialist nationalism became a political and social force of some significance in most major and many small countries of Western Europe in the following decades. In some places, it became, among various other influences, an ideological inspiration and emotional incentive for the green parties and peace movements that emerged in the 1970s and 1980s.

The foremost example was the radical movements in the Federal Republic of Germany. One of their foremost intellectual and emotional sources was the student revolts in the late 1960s, which in Germany were self-consciously ideological and at the same time essentially romantic. Convinced that the existing order of society was totally corrupt, the students rebelled against the well-entrenched liberal tradition and rejected the neocapitalist system of West Germany. Though some adopted the communist model of the Soviet Union, more drew their inspiration from the revolutionary movements of the Third World. In later years some of those students formed ecological groups and helped to start the Green Party, carrying with them a good deal of the ideological baggage of 1967–8.

The Greens, who formed a political party in 1979, entered Parliament four years later and soon gained a substantial representation, drawing their support mainly from the younger generation. Notwithstanding their environmental concerns and global outlook, they became, on balance, a nationalist rather than an internationalist influence in German politics. Their nationalism, typically based on pacifist and anticapitalist doctrines and antimilitarist and anti-Americanist sentiments, was very much leftist. So was the nationalism of the German peace movements, which reached their peak in the earlier 1980s. Their demonstrations, launched in protest against, in particular, the deployment of certain missiles and in general the continuation of the arms race, were aimed mainly at NATO and the United States.

Alarmed by the risks of a continued superpower rivalry, the leaders and supporters of the movements questioned the West German commitment to the West and mooted the alternative course of unification with East Germany and neutrality in the East–West conflict.

The nationalist ideas and sentiments of the Greens and the peace movement spread to the left wing of the Social Democratic Party (SPD). While the Greens established close links with the SPD, the peace movement attracted the support of many of its younger members. Meanwhile the left wing, in particular the youth organization, was reviving the Marxist tradition in an attempt to radicalize the party. Thus, the novel radical concerns became linked with traditional socialist goals. As a result, a nationalism that was marked by rejection of the capitalist system, aversion to the West and cultivation of the Third World gained ground. Within sections of the SPD, it expressed itself after 1979 in a growing opposition to NATO strategy, ever-stronger tendencies toward neutralism in East–West conflict and unilateralism in arms control. One outcome of this shift of opinion was a rising pressure on Helmut Schmidt to pursue détente in relations with the German Democratic Republic (DDR) and other East European states.

In some small countries, too, the nationalism of radical socialists influenced the left wing of the social democratic parties and, in the later decades of the cold war, affected the foreign policy of the government. Here Denmark may serve as an example. Socialist nationalism, which first made its mark in Danish parliamentary and public debate in the 1960s was mainly characteristic of some members of the Socialist People's Party, founded by Aksel Larsen the former leader of the Communist Party, after his excommunication by Moscow in 1958, and of the Left Socialists, a break-away group of the Socialist People's Party. It found expression not least in the programs and statements of various, largely leftist or left-of-center, grassroots movements of the same kind as in West Germany. As nationalism goes, it was, like Danish social democratic nationalism, very much on the reactive and defensive side. Conditioned by the oppressive effects of incessant superpower rivalry and provoked by the more demanding forms of Western cooperation, it was directed essentially at the policies of NATO and the federalist tendencies of the EC, both of which were seen as threats to the sovereign rights, political interests and traditional values of Denmark. Commensurate with the multidimensional quality of the perceived threats, such nationalism took political and economic as well as cultural forms.

As an inspiration of antimilitarist and potentially neutralist criticism of the leadership, policies and practices of NATO, Danish socialist nationalism often had an anti-American character. When motivating anticapitalist opposition to membership of the EC or to the programs and objectives of the institution, it initially displayed anti-German and occasionally even anti-Catholic elements but later revealed pronounced feelings against all the great powers and multinational corporations as well as against Europe in general. As in Germany, such nationalism carried the progressive label, being linked with neo-radical concerns about peace, the Third World and the global environment. Its political influence was probably strongest in the 1980s, when it had affected the left wing of the SDP. Having gone into opposition, this party found itself interacting with the Socialist People's Party and the Radical Liberals in opposing the NATO and EC policies of the minority coalition government of right-of-center parties. The result was a shift toward the left in social democratic policy, and the passing of a large number of parliamentary resolutions that qualified and restricted the alliance and Community policies of the government.

The reduction of tension in Europe and progress in arms control in the late 1980s, followed by the termination of the cold war in the early 1990s, led to a decline of this kind of socialist nationalism in Western Europe. The peace movements went into retreat, while the Greens, who owed their origins in large part to the antinuclear protests in the earlier 1980s, suffered a reversal of fortune. The parliamentary campaigns against NATO conducted by socialists and leftist social democrats, too, lost much of their impetus. However, while the collapse of the Soviet Union, the disappearance of the WTO and the lowering of NATO's profile in the political landscape had removed some major incentives to such nationalism, the pressures for further integration of the EC remained. Thus, the single most important target of socialist nationalists in the 1990s became the sustained efforts of EC enthusiasts to develop a multidimensional EU.

Most of the parties and groups displaying such nationalist inclinations were against the proposed development of the EU because they thought it would go too far and transgress the rights, interests and values of member states. Some, however, opposed it because they believed it might not go far enough in meeting the high standards already achieved by various members in particular fields, such as social legislation and ecological regulation. The most striking manifestations of such diverse reactions to the EU were probably the results produced by the various national referenda, whether on the Maastricht treaty or on proposals for joining that institution.

The negative votes in the referenda, however, reflected not only socialist and other leftist attitudes but also lingering social democratic opposition to, or doubts about, the EU. Though most social democrats had long since come around to the view that their social and economic goals could be pursued more effectively through European cooperation and integration than through isolated national efforts, some of them, not only on the Left but also from other sections of the parties, had still not overcome their nationalist inhibitions toward the Community. But, to the extent that social democratic nationalism originally had been provoked by the conduct of NATO and the pursuit of East–West rivalry, it was checked by the revolutionary events in global and regional politics at the outset of the 1990s. The unification of Germany even led to a new determination in some social democratic circles to maintain NATO and keep the Americans involved in European politics. Thus, by the mid-1990s social democratic nationalism, like the socialist version, appeared to be, on balance, on the retreat.

While socialist and social democratic nationalism lost a good deal of their momentum, communist nationalism almost disappeared. Having been directed largely against the Soviet theory and practice of communist internationalism, it was deprived of its *raison d'être* in Eastern Europe when the people's democracies collapsed and the Soviet Union disintegrated. To the extent that nationalist tendencies in the Eurocommunist parties of the West were reactions to ideological doctrines laid down and political control exercised by the Soviet leaders, communist nationalism had no real future there either after these events. But the most compelling reason for the retreat of any kind of Eurocommunist nationalism was of course the rapidly declining support for all forms of communism in Western Europe.

While the various sorts of socialist nationalism declined or disappeared, other kinds of nationalism came to the forefront. The elimination of dualistic tension in European politics released much pent-up liberal nationalism, often secessionist, in countries that for generations had been under communist rule, in particular Yugoslavia and the Soviet Union. Here and there it also opened the way for conservative types of self-assertive and sometimes expansionistic nationalism. In some places, especially Russia, such nationalism frequently also had a communist element, and in other places, notably the Balkans, it usually had religious overtones. While the enduring social democratic and socialist nationalism acted as brakes on further integration of Western Europe and consolidation of the EU, the emergent liberal and conservative nationalism became factors in the breakup of multinational states and the eruption of violent conflict in parts of Russia and the Balkans.

Conclusion

The overall development in European politics since the early 1990s has been marked by ideological convergence. The extremes on both the right and the left of the political spectrum have faded or disappeared. While solidarist conservative internationalism, associated in particular with the early years of the EEC, has long since retired into comparative obscurity and the pluralist version, manifested primarily in NATO, has been kept in the background most of the time, communist socialist internationalism has disappeared as a political force and the social democratic version has lost some of its strength. Though resurgent or new nationalisms of various kinds have asserted themselves in parts of Europe, they have usually been local phenomena rather than manifestations of general tendencies. The major ideological forces have been a rampant liberal, a somewhat subdued social democratic and an intermittent pluralist conservative internationalism on one side, and traditional conservative and lingering socialist and social democratic nationalisms on the other side. Thus, the stage has been set for a rivalry between the remaining internationalisms and antagonism between them and the prevailing nationalisms.

Whether a balance between internationalism and nationalism can be reached that will be stable enough to maintain a Europeanism sufficiently solid and durable to support a monetary union and, in the more distant future, also some kind of political union, or whether the outcome of the interaction between the two sets of ideological trends will be a strengthening of nationalist tendencies and an accentuation of diplomatic dissension within Europe, may depend primarily on powerful forces at work in the wider world and on the way Europeans perceive them. At the beginning of the twenty-first century the most sweeping forces in world politics seem to be mainly transnational in character.

If European governments and peoples see current trends in global commerce, finance, transport and communication, reinforced as they are by rapidly developing technological facilities and largely dominated by the United States, as constituting serious threats to European interests and values, and if they believe it possible to protect themselves against some of the effects of such trends, the result may be a revival or strengthening of Europeanism. The *raison d'être* of a protective Europeanism, which would be likely to have a substantial element of social democratic internationalism, might be to safeguard the economic, social and cultural achievements of the past against the global market forces of the future.

Conversely, if Europeans do not see those global trends as real threats or find it impossible to protect themselves against the dangers involved, they seem less likely to serve as incentives to a strengthening of Europeanism. Indeed, if such trends seemed to offer economic advantages or diplomatic opportunities for certain European countries but not for others, they might even help to stimulate nationalist tendencies and to provoke political disagreement within Europe. If the protective reaction envisaged in the former scenario is likely to be more typical of leftist or left-of-center parties, the possible attitudes indicated here might be more characteristic of parties on the right or right-of-center of the political spectrum.

However, the powerful transnational forces in the contemporary world are not all of the US-led economic, financial and technological kind usually referred to collectively as globalization. The recent acts of terrorism in New York and Washington, which shocked the United States and most other nations, demonstrated that anti-Western enmity and religious fundamentalism have become forces of primary importance in global politics. The immediate reaction to the events of 11 September 2001, was to form an alliance with the aims of bringing the perpetrators to justice and punishing the governments of countries harboring terrorist groups. Led by the United States with Britain as junior partner, the alliance enjoyed from the outset a degree of support from most European governments, not only those of NATO members but also Russia's, as well as the approval of many other nations in the world, even a considerable number of Arab states. The internationalism manifested in that broad alliance was largely conservative, being directed against revolutionary forces and motivated by security concerns. Viewed in a narrow European perspective, it could be seen as a sudden resurgence of conservative internationalism in a pan-European form. But, in reality, it was more a case of the current ideological rivalries in European politics being superseded for a while by a sweeping diplomatic and strategic response to a sudden challenge from anti-Western transnational terrorist organizations.

If war against Taliban forces in Afghanistan and their supporters from other Islamic countries, fails to produce the desired results, and perhaps spreads to other countries deemed guilty of sheltering terrorist groups, international support for the alliance is likely to dwindle rapidly and opposition to American policies and British involvement to grow, possibly even in the event of further terrorist attacks being launched against Western powers. Such a development would also affect European attitudes, at governmental as well as public levels. The implications for Europeanist ideology and integrationist efforts could be various. If not only public opinion but also the governments of Europe came around to the view that American attempts to stamp out terrorism and punish "rogue states" presented a substantial danger to the peace of the world and the interests of Europe, opposition to US policies might be a unifying influence in the region. On the other hand, if the governments of a few of the major countries and significant sections of public opinion in Europe remained of the view that transnational terrorism was a serious threat that should be resisted with armed force, the effect on European thought and action might be quite divisive. Ultimately, the decisive considerations for the Europeans may be the nature, magnitude and location of any new acts of terrorism, and the durability of this transnational force.

Eventually, however, a situation may arise in which transnational influences and forces, of one kind or another, no longer seem the most salient features of the modern world and intergovernmental relations of high politics once again come to demand priority of consideration. One conceivable, though on present indications not very likely, scenario is a resurgent Russia adopting forceful policies toward some of its neighbors and straining its relations with the United States, and consequently finding itself again involved in a dualistic conflict with the world's strongest power. Another possibility is of regional conflict, whether in West Asia, East Asia or the Subcontinent, leading to a more complex system of interaction, with several great powers rivaling each other. The rising tension and recurrent crises usually associated with such developments would be likely to condition European political thought significantly. If the dynamics of great-power rivalry, global or regional, put new pressures on Europe, the result might be a strengthening of Europeanist tendencies, as in Western Europe in the cold war. Since, in such circumstances, the principal concern presumably once again would be security, any resurgent Europeanism might be characterized by conservative more than by liberal and social democratic internationalism.

The balance between internationalism and nationalism in Europe, and perhaps even the balances among the various kinds of each of those ideologies, may be conditioned by international and transnational forces at work in the states system at large. But the actual nature and real influence of any Europeanism that may emerge from such balances will be determined by the relative strength and complex interaction of political forces operating within Europe itself, and within each of its countries. Whether regional, local, national or sectional, such forces are of many kinds and fluctuating influence. Thus, the ideological composition and political viability of any future Europeanism must remain unpredictable. But, whatever character it may assume and influence it may acquire, such Europeanism is likely to represent a compromise between commitment to internationalist goals and respect for national rights, as long as the states that make up Europe retain a degree of national sovereignty. It may always be the ideology of unity in diversity.

In its external aspects, Europeanism, like other cases of political regionalism, is bound to present some ambivalence. While to its supporters it is open and constructive, to outsiders it can seem closed and defensive. From one point of view an inspiring example of regional internationalism, from another angle it may appear more as an expression of collective nationalism.

Both tracing the historical patterns of European international political thought and speculating about future tendencies point to the conclusion that such thought cannot be explained merely in terms of regional forces and influences. It is conditioned by the structure and processes of the states system at large and influenced by the ideological trends prevailing in the world beyond Europe. Reflecting the rise of non-European great powers and the expansion of international society, extra-European conditions and influences have become increasingly important during the last century, especially since WWII. In recent decades the strongest pressures and influences have come from the United States. This seems likely to be the case for a long time to come.

The present study also demonstrates that it is possible to penetrate the complexity of the politics of modern and contemporary Europe by identifying and examining the various strands of the international political thought of the region, tracing their course through history and observing their interaction in changing international and national circumstances. International thought, like other political thinking, reflects historical experience and projects political goals. Linking the past with the future, it is a summary of knowledge and interpretation as well as an inspiration and guide to action. Combining what people and nations make of their history with what they want for their future, it is the ideological force in their political life. Thus, to focus on the nature, development and influence of the international thought of the region is to go to the heart of the history and politics of Europe.

In this perspective, the last two hundred years of European international politics may be seen as having been shaped largely by two very broad patterns of thought, internationalism and nationalism. Their influence has grown stronger during the last century, which in Europe, as in many other parts of the world, has been a period of international organization. It is this process in particular that has been determined by the tension between the two opposed ideologies. Their interaction has become more intense in the last half century, when the institutionalization of international relations, starting with the economic and military organizations of Western and Eastern Europe and reaching its most advanced point with the EU, has been the dominant characteristic of European politics. For a long time to come, it seems safe to predict, the pressures of the two sets of ideological forces will determine the nature and condition the activities of the EU.

While the European internationalism of the mid-twentieth century to some extent appeared in reaction to the nationalism that had marred earlier decades, the nationalism of the later part of the century emerged to a large extent in opposition to prevailing internationalism and resistance to its organizational manifestations. To conceive of nationalism as not merely an outcome of particular social and political circumstances on the domestic scene but also as a reaction or challenge to certain ideological trends and political developments on the international scene helps the student of international relations to understand the nature of contemporary nationalism and assess its role in European politics. This approach may be particularly useful when applied to a regional system of states engaged in expanding cooperation and advancing integration. But it can also be used with advantage in the analysis of more static situations, such as that of mid-nineteenth century Europe, where long-established conservative internationalist forces were challenged by emergent nationalist movements.

In distinguishing and delineating various forms of internationalism and nationalism in European political thought, the traditional categories of conservative, liberal and socialist thought have proved useful. Having been widely applied in practice as well as theory since the nineteenth century, they are well established in European politics, at both the national and the international level. Indeed, some forms of internationalism and nationalism have for long been known by such labels. Thus, there are recognized traditions of liberal and socialist internationalism and a recurrent pattern of liberal nationalism.

A more important advantage of using the traditional categories is that it allows one to complete and clarify the more common mental pictures of the broad patterns of international political thought. The tendency of most writers interested in internationalist ideas to focus on the liberal or the socialist form raises the question whether there might not be a complementary set of ideas that could be described as conservative internationalism. The present study identifies such a form of internationalism and distinguishes two types, namely pluralist and solidarist conservative thought. It also shows that conservative internationalism, of one kind or another, has been a theme of European thought for several centuries. Similarly, the inclination of students of nationalism to concentrate on liberal and conservative forms gives rise to the question whether there might not be a socialist variety too. This study recognizes such a form, distinguishes three types and shows that socialist nationalism has been a periodically recurrent phenomenon in European politics since the early twentieth century. By establishing that thinkers and actors of the two progressive schools of thought have no monopoly on internationalism and by demonstrating that socialists, too, can be nationalists, the study presents a broader and more complex view of the ideological trends in European history and politics.

Notes

Introduction

1. To separate internationalism from cosmopolitanism is a departure from the traditional usage of the former term. Fred Halliday, in his inaugural lecture at the London School of Economics, noted that past internationalist thought had been evident, and linked, in the ideas of world government and of a universal language. Seeing contemporary internationalism as tied up with the theme of ongoing processes of internationalization of the world, he distinguished three concepts, namely liberal, hegemonic and revolutionary internationalism ("Three Concepts of Internationalism," *International Affairs*, vol. 64, no. 3, spring 1988, pp. 187–98). While each had its own goal and benefits, all of the concepts projected some kind of movement away from the old order of nation-states toward a better, more integrated world. Thus, they may all be classed as progressive.

2. To consider nationalism in the context of international relations represents a departure from traditional practice in the vast literature on the subject. While sociologists and political scientists have usually studied nationalism as a phenomenon arising from and, in turn, affecting domestic social and political conditions, this study presents it more as a reaction or challenge to circumstances prevailing in international society. To the extent that the causes and effects of nationalism are discussed here, they are considered primarily in their international dimension. However, the focus is generally on the ideology itself and its interaction with internationalism.

Chapter One. Conservative Internationalism

1. The term is Martin Wight's. For a distinction between periods of balance-of-power politics and periods of doctrinal conflict in European history, see his *Power Politics*, ed. H. Bull and C. Holbraad (Harmondsworth: Penguin, 1979), chap. 7 and app. II.

2. Hansard, 3rd ser., clv, col. 1225 (8 August, 1859). For an analysis of the ideas of Castlereagh, Palmerston, Russell and Gladstone on the balance of power, see C. Holbraad, *The Concert of Europe. A Study in German and British International Theory 1815–1914* (London: Longman, 1970), pp. 136–48.

3. Ibid., pp. 148–52.

4. Ibid., pp. 15–34.

5. L. von Ranke, *Ueber die Epochen der neueren Geschichte*, ed. A. Dove (Leipzig: Duncker, 1888), pp. 204–5. For an analysis of the ideas of Gentz, Ancillon, Heeren and Ranke about the balance of power, see Holbraad, *The Concert of Europe*, pp. 16–23, 36–8 and 81–9.

6. Holbraad, *The Concert of Europe*, pp. 90–107.

7. G. Egerton, "Conservative Internationalism: British Approaches to International Organization and the Creation of the League of Nations," in *Diplomacy and Statecraft*, vol. 5, no. 1 (March 1994), pp. 1–20.

8. M. M. Ball, *NATO and the European Union Movement* (London: Stevens and Sons, 1959), p. 3.

9. J. Monnet, *Memoirs*, trans. R. Mayne (London: Collins, 1978), p. 432.

10. Ibid., p. 441.

11. *My Life in Politics*, trans. A. Bell (London: Hamish Hamilton, 1992), p. 243.

12. Robert Aron, *An Explanation of de Gaulle* (New York: Harper and Row, 1966), p. 188.

13. M. Light, *The Soviet Theory of International Relations* (Brighton: Wheatsheaf Books, 1988), p. 202.

14. Ibid., p. 305.

15. Ibid., p. 197.

16. Ibid., pp. 305–8.

17. E. A. Carrillo, *Alcide De Gasperi. The Long Apprenticeship* (University of Notre Dame Press, 1965), pp. 127–9.

18. P. Weymar, *Konrad Adenauer. The Authorized Biography*, trans. P. de Mendelssohn (London: Andre Deutsch, 1957), p. 13.

19. Ibid., p. 197.

20. "Don't forget," Adenauer told the French High Commissioner in 1954, "that I am the only German Chancellor who has preferred the unity of Europe to the unity of his own country." (R. Augstein, *Konrad Adenauer*, trans. W. Wallich (London: Secker and Warburg, 1964), p. 77.)

21. Light, *The Soviet Theory of International Relations*, p. 190; the writer quoted was Kuusinen.

22. Ibid., p. 191.

Chapter Two. Liberal Internationalism

1. *Hansard's Parliamentary Debates*, 3rd ser., cxii, col. 673 (28 June).

2. "Vindication of the French Revolution of February 1848," in J. S. Mill, *Dissertations and Discussions, Political, Philosophical, and Historical*, vol. ii (London: Parker, 1859), pp. 379–81.

3. P. S. Wandycz, "Liberal Internationalism. The Contribution of British and French Liberal Thought to the Theory of International Relations," unpublished Ph.D. thesis, University of London, 1950, p. 136.

4. Holbraad, *The Concert of Europe*, pp. 176–98.

5. For Hobson's contribution to liberal internationalism, see D. Long, *Towards a New Liberal Internationalism. The International Theory of J. A. Hobson* (Cambridge: Cambridge University Press, 1996).

6. For a brief presentation and critique of Mitrany's political and social thought, see C. Navari, "David Mitrany and International Functionalism," in D. Long and P. Wilson (eds.), *Thinkers of the Twenty Years' Crisis. Inter-war Idealism Reassessed* (Oxford: Clarendon Press, 1995), pp. 214–46.

7. For a reassessment, from a modern liberal internationalist point of view, of the thoughts of British and other writers of the interwar period, which British and American writers of the realist school of the following decades tended to reject as idealist or utopian, see Long and Wilson, *Thinkers of the Twenty Years' Crisis*.

8. "Vindication of the French Revolution of February 1848," in Mill, *Dissertations and Discussions*, vol. ii, pp. 379–81.

9. J. Morley, *The Life of William Ewart Gladstone* (London: Macmillan, 1903), vol. ii, p. 596 (speech of 1879). See also Gladstone's admission in a letter to Granville of 8 October, 1870: "In moral forces, and in their growing effect upon European politics, I have a great faith: possibly on that very account, I am free to confess, sometimes a misleading one." (*The Political Correspondence of Mr. Gladstone and Lord Granville 1868–1876*, ed. A. Ramm, Camden Third Series vols. lxxxi and lxxxii (London: Royal Historical Society, 1952), vol. i, p. 140.)

10. For a survey of the humanitarian internationalism of British liberals in the late nineteenth and early twentieth centuries, see Holbraad, *The Concert of Europe*, pp. 162–76.

11. A relevant distinction here is between the cosmopolitanist and the internationalist form of the domestic analogy. For the history and analysis of this concept, see H. Suganami, *The Domestic Analogy and World Order Proposals* (Cambridge: Cambridge University Press, 1989).

12. Monnet, *Memoirs*, p. 222 (note of 5 August, 1943).

13. Ibid., pp. 271–3 (letter to George Bidault).

14. Ibid., pp. 321, 326.

15. Ibid., p. 399.

16. Ibid., p. 353.

17. Ibid., pp. 304–5.

18. Ibid., p. 524.

19. Ibid., p. 222.

20. Ibid., pp. 272–3.

21. Ibid., p. 310.

22. Ibid., pp. 399–400.

23. Ibid., p. 442 (the Action Committee's declaration of 26 June); see also p. 466. For a further response to de Gaulle's ideas and policies, see Monnet's letter of February 1963 to friends after the first veto of British membership of the EC, in which he rejects as out-of-date and impossible the plan for a system from the Atlantic to the Urals (p. 460).

24. For the distinction between functionalism and neo-functionalism, see C. Pentland, *International Theory and European Integration* (London: Faber and Faber, 1973), pp. 64–132.

25. A. Spinelli, *The Eurocrats, Conflict and Crisis in The European Community*, trans. C. Grove Haines (Baltimore: The Johns Hopkins Press, 1966), p. 25.

26. M. Burgess, *Federalism and European Union. Political Ideas, Influences and Strategies in the European Community 1972–1987* (London: Routledge, 1989), pp. 55–6.

27. Spinelli, *The Eurocrats*, p. 11.

28. Ibid., pp. 178–9.

29. S. D. Krasner, "Sovereignty, Régimes, and Human Rights," in V. Rittberger (ed.), *Régime Theory and International Relations* (Oxford: Clarendon Press, 1995), pp. 139–67.

Chapter Three. Socialist Internationalism

1. E. Wilson, *To the Finland Station. A Study in the Writing and Acting of History* (London: Martin Secker and Warburg Ltd., 1941), pp. 447–8.

2. In Britain, reformist socialism did not emerge through a revision of Marxism. It had its roots in Christianity and nineteenth-century radical liberalism, and owed much to the social experiments of Robert Owen, the writings of J. S. Mill and the ideas of the Fabian socialists. In various ways, it found expression in the cooperative movement, trade unionism and the chartist movement, and eventually in the establishment of the Labor Party. Throughout its long development, the ideology of British socialism has always been essentially reformist.

3. See part II, chap. 6, pp. 145–52 in this book.

4. Light, *The Soviet Theory of International Relations*, pp. 178–9.

5. Ibid., p. 176; see also V. Kubalkova and A. A. Cruikshank, *Marxism and International Relations* (Oxford: Clarendon Press, 1985), pp. 94–5, 190.

6. Light, *The Soviet Theory of International Relations*, p. 194.

7. Ibid., pp. 183–4.

8. For a discussion of the communist conception of human rights, see R. J. Vincent, *Human Rights and International Relations* (Cambridge: Cambridge University Press, 1986), pp. 61–4.

9. G. Stern, *The Rise and Decline of International Communism* (Aldershot: Edward Elgar, 1990), pp. 229–30.

10. For the origin of the term Eurocommunism, see W. Laqueur, *A Continent Astray: Europe, 1970–1978* (Oxford: Oxford University Press, 1979), p. 87; for a discussion of the phenomenon, see also Kubalkova and Cruickshank, *Marxism and International Relations*, pp. 124–6.

11. Brandt, *My Life in Politics*, p. 416.

12. Ibid., p. 423.

13. Ibid., p. 313.

14. Ibid., p. 424.
15. Ibid., pp. 314–17.
16. Ibid., p. 317.
17. Ibid., pp. 404–7.
18. See part I, chap. 1, pp. 24–6 in this book.
19. Article 3 (i).

Chapter Four. Conservative Nationalism

1. For a brief analysis of the nature and influence of Hegelian ideas in nineteenth-century German thought about European politics and for a survey of the confluence of various strands of German thought in the later part of the century, see Holbraad, *The Concert of Europe*, pp. 72–113.

2. For an account of romanticism and nationalism in early nineteenth-century Germany and of German conservative nationalism after 1918, see H. Kohn, *The Mind of Germany. The Education of a Nation* (London: Macmillan, 1961), chaps. 3, 4, 11, 12.

3. W. A. Phillips, *The Confederation of Europe. A Study of the European Alliance, 1813–1823 as an Experiment in the International Organization of Peace* (London: Longmans, 1914), p. 278.

4. For a brief discussion of the nationalist and imperialist strand of thought and its roots in earlier British ideas about European politics, see Holbraad, *The Concert of Europe*, pp. 198–204.

5. J. K. Chalaby, "Twenty Years of Contrast: The French and British Press during the Inter-War Period," in *European Journal of Sociology*, vol. xxxvii (1996), pp. 143–59.

6. D. Cook, *Charles de Gaulle: A Biography* (London: Secker and Warburg, 1984), title page.

7. Ibid., p. 333. In de Gaulle's vocabulary, "Anglo-Saxon" meant British-American.

8. Quoted in Monnet, *Memoirs*, p. 441.

9. For a study of Margaret Thatcher's ideas on foreign policy, see C. Coker, *Who Only England Know. The Conservatives and Foreign Policy*, Institute for European Defence & Strategic Studies, occasional paper no. 47 (London, 1990).

10. C. M. Woodhouse, *Modern Greece. A Short History* (London: Faber and Faber, 1977), p. 308.

11. W. O. Henderson, *The Genesis of the Common Market* (London: Frank Cass & Co., 1962), p. 141.

12. For the relationship between nationalism and international society in general, and the consequences of the former for the latter in particular, see J. Mayall, *Nationalism and International Society* (Cambridge: Cambridge University Press, 1990).

Chapter Five. Liberal Nationalism

1. C. J. H. Hayes, *The Historical Evolution of Modern Nationalism* (New York: Macmillan, 1948), p. 155, quoted in Wandycz, "Liberal Internationalism," p. 283.
2. H. Kohn, *Prophets and Peoples. Studies in Nineteenth Century Nationalism* (New York: The Macmillan Company, 1947), p. 50.
3. Ibid., p. 50.
4. Wandycz, "Liberal Internationalism," p. 138.
5. Ibid., pp. 291–5.
6. See above, pp. 136–8.
7. Kohn, *The Mind of Germany*, p. 135.
8. J. G. Droysen, *Politische Schriften*, ed. F. Gilbert (Munich: Oldenbourg, 1933), p. 122; see also pp. 217–19.
9. Ibid., p. 59; see also pp. 136, 229.
10. H. von Treitschke, *Politik*, ed. M. Cornicelius (Leipzig: Hirzel, 1897–8) vol. i, p. 73; vol. ii, p. 518.
11. Ibid., vol. i, p. 72; see also p. 30.
12. F. Naumann, *Demokratie und Kaisertum. Ein Handbuch für innere Politik* (Berlin-Schöneberg: "Hilfe", 1905), pp. 206–7.
13. Kohn, *The Mind of Germany*, pp. 278–87.
14. L. Dehio, *Germany and World Politics in the Twentieth Century*, trans. D. Pevsner (London: Chatto & Windus, 1959), pp. 85–9; and Holbraad, *The Concert of Europe*, pp. 101–4.
15. See part I, chap. 2, p. 41 in this book.
16. P. Brock, "Polish Nationalism," in P. F. Sugar and I. J. Lederer, *Nationalism in Eastern Europe* (Seattle: University of Washington Press, 1969), p. 369.
17. G. Barany, "Hungary: From Aristocratic to Proletarian Nationalism," in Sugar and Lederer, *Nationalism in Eastern Europe*, pp. 302–3.
18. C. Holbraad, "Denmark: Half-Hearted Partner," in N. Ørvik (ed.), *Semi-alignment and Western Security* (London: Croom Helm, 1986) pp. 15–60.
19. C. Melakopides, "Greece: From Compliance to Self-Assertion," in Ørvik, *Semialignment and Western Security*, pp. 61–8.
20. C. Holbraad, *Danish Neutrality. A Study in the Foreign Policy of a Small State* (Oxford: Clarendon Press, 1991), pp. 152–8.

Chapter Six. Socialist Nationalism

1. Quoted in K. N. Waltz, *Man, the State and War. A Theoretical Analysis* (New York: Columbia University Press, 1959), p. 143.
2. M. V. Pundeff, "Bulgarian Nationalism," in Sugar and Lederer, *Nationalism in Eastern Europe*, pp. 162–3.
3. Ibid., pp. 163–4.
4. S. Fischer-Galati, "Romanian Nationalism," in Sugar and Lederer, *Nationalism in Eastern Europe*, p. 394.

5. Quoted in Fischer-Galati, "Romanian Nationalism," p. 373.

6. For analyses of Polish nationalism in the postwar decades, see P. Brock, "Polish Nationalism," in Sugar and Lederer, *Nationalism in Eastern Europe*, pp. 365–72, and Stern, *The Rise and Decline of International Communism*, pp. 196–200.

7. From a speech by Gomulka on 4 November, 1956, quoted in Brock, "Polish Nationalism," p. 370.

8. Laqueur, *A Continent Astray*, p. 89.

9. For a survey of the emergence and analysis of the phenomenon of Eurocommunism, see ibid., chap. 4.

10. Henderson, *The Genesis of the Common Market*, p. 141.

11. Quoted in C. Tugendhat, *Making Sense of Europe* (Harmondsworth: Viking, 1986), p. 34.

12. Laqueur, *A Continent Astray*, p. 121.

13. Monnet, *Memoirs*, p. 319.

14. Spinelli, *The Eurocrats*, p. 185.

15. For a detailed study of Danish qualifications to the policies and divergences from the programs of NATO, see Holbraad, "Denmark: Half-Hearted Partner," in Ørvik, *Semialignment and Western Security*, pp. 15–60.

16. For a survey and analysis of Danish policy toward the EC, see Holbraad, *Danish Neutrality*, pp. 114–18, 152–68.

17. For a discussion of the change in social democratic orientations after German unification, see ibid., pp. 169–74.

18. For a bitter critique of the Norwegian Labour Party's security policy in the NATO period, see N. Ørvik, "Norway: Deterrence versus Nonprovocation," in Ørvik, *Semialignment and Western Security*, pp. 186–247.

19. J. J. Holst, "The New Europe: A View from the North," lecture to Fundacion Jose Ortega y Gasset, Madrid, 29 October, 1991, p. 18 of unpublished text.

20. For a sympathetic analysis of the security and alliance policy of Greece in the NATO period, see C. Melakopides, "Greece: From Compliance to Self-Assertion," in Ørvik, *Semialignment and Western Security*, pp. 61–106; for a brief study of Greece's relations with the EC, see J. Pettifer, "Greek Polity and the European Community, 1974–1993," in Ph. Carabott (ed.), *Greece and Europe in the Modern Period: Aspects of a Troubled Relationship* (London: Centre for Hellenic Studies, King's College London, 1995), pp. 96–106.

21. For a study of Greece in contemporary Europe, see S. Economides, "Greece and the New Europe in the 1990s," in Carabott, *Greece and Europe*, pp. 107–30.

22. For an analysis of Swedish security policy in the first twenty-five years of the cold war, see N. Andrén, "Sweden's Security Policy," in J. J. Holst (ed.), *Five Roads to Nordic Security* (Oslo: Universitetsforlaget, 1973), pp. 127–53.

23. For case studies in support of such generalizations, see the chapters on Denmark and Norway in Ørvik, *Semialignment and Western Security*.

Biographical Glossary

Adenauer, Konrad (1876–1967). Christian Democratic chancellor of the Federal Republic of Germany (1949–63), who played a major role in integrating West Germany with the West in the cold war, which culminated with the accession to NATO in 1955, in setting up the European Communities of the 1950s and in establishing a special relationship with de Gaulle's France.

Alexander I (1777–1825). Tsar of Russia (1801–25), who joined coalitions against France and Napoleon and became a leading figure at the Congress of Vienna during 1814–15. Together with the rulers of Austria and Prussia, he set up the Holy Alliance of the Christian sovereigns of Continental Europe. Partly as a result of the influence of Metternich, the Austrian chancellor, his liberal ideas gave way to reactionary policies in the postwar decade.

Angell, Ralph Norman (1872–1967). English economist, writer and worker for international peace, who wrote more than forty books. The best known is *The Great Illusion* (1910 and several later editions), in which he argued that war and conquest did not bring a nation economic advantages. Of long-established radical liberal views, he joined the Labor Party after WWI. In the 1930s he supported policies of collective security against aggressors. He was awarded the Nobel Peace Prize (1933).

Bernstein, Edward (1850–1932). German socialist writer, who criticized established Marxist theory. Born in Berlin, he spent many years in Switzerland and also in London, where he met Marx and Engels as well as some early Fabian reformist socialists. He became an influential theorist of socialism, arguing that the way forward lay through reform of the existing social system rather than its overthrow. His "revisionism" was denounced by many German Social Democrats and other Continental socialists, not least Lenin, all of whom believed in the revolutionary dictatorship of the proletariat.

Brandt, Willy (1913–92). Leader of the SPD from 1961 and chancellor of the Federal Republic of Germany (1969–74), who played a major role in relations between West and East in German and European politics. He fled from

Nazi Germany to Scandinavia in the 1930s, took Norwegian citizenship and returned to Germany in 1945. Serving as mayor of Berlin (1957–66), he was influential in the drawing up of the Bad Gödesberg Program of 1959, in which the SPD renounced its Marxist heritage. As foreign minister (1966–9), he recognized, negotiated with and visited the German Democratic Republic. After a spy scandal that involved one of his assistants, he resigned as chancellor. Later he chaired the Independent Commission on International Development Issues that produced the Brandt Report in 1980. He was awarded the Nobel Peace Prize (1971).

Castlereagh, Robert Stewart (1769–1822). British foreign secretary (1812–22), who played an important role in guiding the Grand Alliance against Napoleonic France, deciding the form of the Vienna peace settlement of 1815 and setting up the congress system of postwar European diplomacy. He was considerably more European in outlook than his successor George Canning.

Cobden, Richard (1804–65). English writer and politician of radical liberal convictions. Two of his most influential pamphlets were *England, Ireland, and America* (1835) and *Russia* (1836), in which he argued against the principle of the balance of power and the practice of foreign armed intervention and for free trade among nations. Prominent among the advocates of the repeal of the Corn Laws in the 1840s, he became, together with John Bright, a leader of the Manchester School, part of the program of which was a reduction in national armaments and an end to imperial expansion.

Delors, Jacques Lucien Jean (b. 1925). French civil servant, politician and European statesman, who championed the development of the EU. Having joined the Socialist Party in 1973, he became party spokesman on EEC monetary affairs. After two years as member of the European Parliament, he became a minister in Francois Mitterand's government in 1981. As president of the European Commission (1985–94), he was responsible for speeding up the process of European integration and promoting the treaty on EU drawn up at Maastricht in 1991. His insistence on going beyond the economic union of an internal market and seeking also a monetary and political union brought him into conflict with the British government of Margaret Thatcher.

Ellemann-Jensen, Uffe (b. 1941). Danish journalist and politician, who as foreign minister (1982–93) became known as his country's Mr. Europe. Leader of the Liberal Party from 1984, he became vice-president in 1985 and president in 1995 of the European Liberal Party. After a narrow defeat in the general election of 1998, he resigned the leadership of the Liberal Party and later left Danish politics. He was awarded the Robert Schuman Prize (1987).

De Gasperi, Alcide (1881–1954). Italian prime minister (1945–53) and leader of the Christian Democratic Party, who helped to consolidate the new democracy in his country and to lay the foundations for the integration of Western Europe. He steered Italy into NATO, cultivated its relations with the United States and played a major role in the setting up of the ECSC.

Gentz, Friedrich (1764–1832). German publicist, who left his native Prussia in 1802 and settled in Austria, where he gained the ear of Metternich and became secretary general of the post-Napoleonic congresses of the great powers. Increasingly critical of the ideas and results of the French Revolution, he translated Edmund Burke's *Reflections on the Revolution in France* into German. Passionately opposed to Napoleonic expansionism, he published works in defense of the prerevolutionary system of European politics, notably *Fragments upon the Balance of Power in Europe* (trans. 1806). Confidential adviser to the Austrian chancellor, he became secretary to the congresses of Vienna, Aix-la-Chapelle, Troppau, Laibach and Verona, where he helped the rulers of Europe to formulate their conservative policies.

Gladstone, William Ewart (1809–98). British statesman who was Chancellor of the Exchequer under three prime ministers and became prime minister four times (1868–74, 1880–5, 1886 and 1892–4). He started his parliamentary career in 1832 as a member of the Tory Party, when he was under the influence of Robert Peel, but gradually moved toward the liberals, becoming leader of the party and ending up as the Grand Old Man of liberalism. His foreign policies reflected great breadth of vision and strong humanitarian concerns.

Hobson, John Atkinson (1858–1940). English journalist and political activist, who wrote many books about international affairs. Of radical liberal views, he resigned from the Liberal Party in 1916 over the proposed abandonment of free trade and joined the Labor Party in 1924. He was against British involvement in European war on the eve of WWI and critical of the Versailles peace settlement of 1919, especially its economic provisions. In the 1930s, he opposed the British policy of appeasing the European dictators and called for greater involvement of the United States in world politics.

Mazzini, Giuseppe (1805–72). Genoese revolutionary and Italian nationalist, who gained prominence in the movement for Italian unity and liberation known as the Risorgimento. He was a member of Carbonari and founder of Young Italy, both secret revolutionary societies. A passionate republican, he rejected the parliamentary form of government established under monarchical auspices after unification in 1861. His ultimate goal, a republican federation of the world, was inspired by his faith in the brotherhood of man.

Metternich, Clemens (1773–1859). Austrian chancellor (1812–48), who was the foremost conservative statesman in the restoration period of European politics. Having led the Habsburg Monarchy into alliance with Russia against Napoleonic France in 1813, he presided at the Congress of Vienna in 1814–15. Determined to uphold the territorial and dynastic order established by the Vienna settlement, he rejected liberal ideas and suppressed radical movements in all parts of Europe within his control. The revolution of 1848 forced him to resign and escape to England.

Mill, John Stuart (1806–73). English philosopher and economist, who was motivated by the need for social and political reform. Of radical liberal views, he became a critical exponent of the prevailing school of utilitarianist philosophy. Foremost among his contributions to political theory are *On Liberty* (1859) and *Considerations on Representative Government* (1861). He was a major figure in the liberal internationalist tradition of thought and also a considerable influence in some reformist strands of socialist internationalism.

Mitrany, David (1888–1975). Rumanian political scientist, who developed the functionalist theory of international integration. Having come to London in 1912 to study sociology at the London School of Economics, he spent the years of WWI in England. Of liberal internationalist convictions, he associated with both Liberal and Labor intellectuals in postwar Britain, including the Fabians, but remained critical of socialism. Having spent much of the interwar decades in the United States, with periods at Harvard and Princeton, he returned to Britain at the beginning of WWII and joined the Royal Institute of International Affairs. His ideas on functionalism were developed mainly in the early 1930s.

Monnet, Jean (1888–1979). French economist and civil servant, who championed European economic and institutional integration. Having drafted the Monnet Plan of 1945–6 for the reconstruction of postwar France and become special adviser to the liberal Catholic statesman Robert Schuman, he was the principal author of the Schuman Plan of 1950, which proposed the establishment of a supranational institution for the management of the coal and steel industries of Western Europe. Subsequently he was the first chairman of the ECSC (1952–5). In the 1960s he was strongly opposed to president de Gaulle's policies, which he found nationalistic and anti-European. After retirement from public office, he formed the Action Committee for a United States of Europe, which was a pro-integration pressure group.

Palme, Olof Joachim (1927–86). Swedish Social Democratic prime minister (1969–76 and 1982–6), who assumed a high profile in international politics. Under his leadership, the party moved to the left. After losing a general election in 1976, he became more active internationally, leading a mission to South Africa in 1977, serving as member of the commission that produced the Brandt Report on the world economy, chairing an Independent Commission on Disarmament and Security and advocating various peace initiatives in Europe. He was assassinated in Stockholm by an unknown person.

Palmerston, Henry John Temple (1784–1865). British foreign secretary (1830–4, 1835–41 and 1846–51) and prime minister (1855–8 and 1859–65) who defended the balance of power as a principle of foreign policy. Through his long career he went through the entire spectrum of party allegiance, starting as a Tory and ending up as a Liberal. While always ready to defend British interests forcefully, he supported some liberal causes abroad.

Ranke, Leopold von (1795–1886). German historian and professor at the University of Berlin (1825–71), who can be seen as the father of modern historiography. His aim was to show things as they actually had been ("wie es eigentlich gewesen") and his method to examine primary sources critically and impartially. Most of his huge oeuvre was about the European powers and their interaction. He saw the balance of power as a mechanism regulating the struggle among states, thereby sustaining the duality of individuality and unity that characterized the European states system.

Russell, John (1792–1878). British prime minister (1846–52 and 1865–6) and holder of other cabinet posts, who championed electoral reform at home and national liberty abroad. In his younger years he was an outspoken critic of the post-Napoleonic association of great powers, which he saw as a conspiracy of sovereigns. As a Whig and later Liberal, he was more European in his outlook than Palmerston, though less than Castlereagh.

Smith, Adam (1723–90). Scottish social philosopher and professor at the University of Glasgow (1751–63), who was a founding father of the liberal internationalist tradition of thought. In *The Wealth of Nations* (1776), the first comprehensive system of political economy, he argued that unhampered trade and manufacture could lead to a rational division of labor in the world and a reduction of conflict among states.

Spinelli, Altiero (1907–86). Italian left-wing politician and European commissioner (1970–6) who espoused what became known as the neo-functionalist approach to European integration. With a background in communist resistance to fascist rule, he supported the postwar movement for a federalist reorganization of Europe, and disliked the gradualist approach to West European integration that became dominant after 1950. Elected to the European Parliament (1976 and 1979), he became a major architect of the draft treaty on EU.

Thatcher, Margaret Hilda (b. 1925). British Conservative prime minister (1979–90), who defended national sovereignty against the drive toward a united Europe. She entered Parliament in 1959, held junior and cabinet posts in the early 1960s and early 1970s and became leader of the party in 1975. In foreign policy she leaned upon the United States, cultivating the "special relationship" between the two principal English-speaking powers. Her ideology, a mixture of conservative nationalism, free-market economics and reliance on strong defense, became known as "Thatcherism." After losing the leadership of the party and joining the House of Lords, she became increasingly anti-European in her opposition to Eurocratic pressures for a monetary and political Union.

Togliatti, Palmiro (1893–1964). Italian Communist leader, who espoused the doctrine, known as polycentrism, of each Communist Party taking its own road to socialism. Having studied together and worked with Antonio Gramsci in his youth and served in the International Brigade in the Spanish Civil War (1936–9), he became a member and subsequently vice secretary of Comintern. After the defeat of fascism, he was elected secretary general of the Italian Communist Party (1944 and 1949). Believing in socialist revolution by electoral means, he served in several postwar governments. Retaining the leadership of the party up to his death, he transformed it into the largest nonrevolutionary Communist Party in the non-Soviet-controlled world.

Index